John Thomas Blight

Churches of West Cornwall

With Notes of Antiquities of the District. Second Edition

John Thomas Blight

Churches of West Cornwall
With Notes of Antiquities of the District. Second Edition

ISBN/EAN: 9783337016869

Printed in Europe, USA, Canada, Australia, Japan

Cover: Foto ©Andreas Hilbeck / pixelio.de

More available books at **www.hansebooks.com**

CHURCHES

OF

WEST CORNWALL;

WITH

Notes of Antiquities of the District.

BY THE LATE J. T. BLIGHT,
AUTHOR OF "A WEEK AT THE LAND'S END."

SECOND EDITION.

Parker and Co.
OXFORD, AND 6 SOUTHAMPTON-STREET,
STRAND, LONDON.
1885.

ADVERTISEMENT

TO THE SECOND EDITION.

IN issuing a Second Edition, which has been called for, the Publishers have only to state that with scarcely any exception the previous Edition, as finally corrected by Mr. Blight from the papers which he contributed to the "Gentleman's Magazine," has been scrupulously followed.

By Mr. Blight's death Archæology has lost not only an enthusiastic student, but a hard worker, and it is much to be feared that his too eager devotion to his favourite pursuit amidst his daily toil brought on the illness which had so sad a termination.

OXFORD,
October, 1884.

PREFACE

TO THE FIRST EDITION.

IN presenting these papers in a collected form, little more need be said than that they were originally published in successive numbers of the "Gentleman's Magazine," during the years 1862—1864. They are reprinted without alteration, with the exception of the concluding remarks of the ninth chapter, which have been re-written; and several notes and woodcuts have been added.

There is still a wide field for investigation among the pre-historic antiquities of the county; but hitherto attention has been directed almost entirely to these, to the exclusion of the ecclesiastical buildings of the Middle Ages. When the county histories were written nothing was known of Church architecture, and it is needless to say that the occasional descriptions of churches which they contain are wholly untrustworthy, and, indeed, quite valueless. Late Norman work is called "Saxon;" late Perpendicular figures as "Early English;" and one writer of eminence assumes the present church at St. German's to be the ancient "cathedral of Cornwall" itself, before Leofric, dilating on the great antiquity of certain windows with geometrical tracery in particular.

Of the thirty-five churches noticed in the following pages, nearly all are of early date, as a careful investigation will prove; but in most of them the early character of the work has been greatly obscured by extensive alterations and additions during the Perpendicular period. And yet, as the illustrations will shew, the Cornish churches are by no means so devoid of interest as is commonly supposed.

The last chapter is occupied by an illustrated narrative of two days' pleasant wandering among the old stones of West Cornwall, in company with the members of the Cambrian Archæological Association.

J. T. B.

PENZANCE,
March, 1865.

From the Rood-screen, St. Burian.

CONTENTS.

	PAGE
DEANERY of St. BURIAN	1
The Church of St. BURIAN	5

Engravings. The Font.—Two arcades from the Rood-screen.—Carving from the Roodscreen, (*see* p. vi.).—The Misereres.—Capital and Base of Pier.—The Tomb of Clarice de Bolleit.

The Church of St. LEVAN 15

Engravings. The Stoup.—Carvings on Bench-ends.—West View of Transept.—Plan of Transept.—Interior of Transept.—Capitals of Piers.—The Font.

The Church of St. SENNEN 21

Engravings. A Capital.—Mutilated Image of the Virgin.

The Church of St. MADRON 24

Engravings. The Font.—The Sedile and Piscina.—A Tower Window.—The Tower Cornice.—Alabaster figures of Angels.

The Church of St. PAUL, near Penzance . . 31

Engravings. Arch between Nave and North Aisle.—The Tower.—The Belfry Windows.

The Church of SANCREED 38

Engraving. Panels of the Roodscreen.

The Church of St. JUST in Penwith . . . 40

Engravings. Two Capitals.—Hoodmould.—Tooth-moulding.—Inscribed Stone.

The Church of St. CURY 45

Engravings. South Doorway.—Hagioscope.—Plan of ditto.—Exterior of Low-side Window.

	PAGE
The Church of GUNWALLOE	50

Engravings. General View of Church.—Fragment of Font.

The Church of MULLION	54

Engravings. The Carving of the Crucifix in the Tower.—Corbel-head.—Stoup.—A Series of eleven Carvings from the Bench-ends.—Carving on the Altar.

The Church of ST. KEVERNE . . .	62

Engravings. A Capital and Base.—Plan of the Church.—Twenty-four Subjects from the Carvings of the Bench-ends.

The Church of ST. MANACCAN . . .	67

Engravings. Plan of the Church.—Piscina.—Interior of Chancel.—South-east View of Chancel and Transept.—South Doorway.

The Church of ST. MAWGAN IN TERRIER . .	72

Engravings. The Hagioscope.—Two Sepulchral Effigies.—Carving on Key-stone of Tower Window.—Shields carved on the Tower.—Jamb of Tower Door.—Key-stone of Tower Arch.

The Church of ST. ANTONY IN KIRRIER . .	78

Engravings. General View of the Church.—Window of Chancel.—East Window of Aisle.—The Font.

The Church of LANDEWEDNACK . . .	82

Engravings. Plan of the Church.—Exterior of Low-side Window.—Boss on the Porch.—South Doorway.—The Font.—Inscription on ditto.—Devices on Bells.

Church of ST. RUAN MAJOR	89

Engravings. Window in South Aisle.—Device on Rood-screen.—Triangular notching.—Plan of Church.—Openings at Junction of Chancel and Nave.—View of Tower.

Church of ST. RUAN MINOR	95

Engravings. The Piscina.—The Font.

Church of ST. GRADE	97

CONTENTS. ix

                                                                                      PAGE

Church of ST. WENDRON 99
    Engravings. Plan of the Church.—Moulding of Arch.—North-east View of Chancel and Transept.—East Window of Chancel.—East Window of Transept.—Capital of Transept Pier.—Capital and Base-mouldings of Pier.—Hood-moulding.—Piscina in Aisle.—The Font.—Capping of Tower Buttress.—Brass.—Incised Stone.

Church of ST. BREAGE 109
    Engravings. An old Helmet in the Church.—Three Capitals.—Cross.

Church of ST. GERMOE 114
    Engravings. General View of Church.—Gable-cross of Porch.—Gable-corbels of Porch.—The Font.—'St. Germoe's Chair.'

Church of ST. PERRAN-UTHNOE . . . 121
    Engravings. Corbel of Tower-arch.—Key-stone of South Doorway.

Church of ST. GULVAL 124
    Engravings. The Credence.—Pinnacle of Tower.—Pier of Tower-arch.—Shields on the Font.

Church of ST. LUDGVAN . . . 127

Church of ST. ERTH 128
    Engravings. Window of North Aisle.—String-course of Tower.

Church of LELANT 129
    Engraving. Capital and Base of Norman Pier.

Church of ST. GWINEAR 130
    Engravings. Plan of the Church.—Window of Chancel.—The Piscina.—Beak-head from Porch.—Corbel-heads from Tower.—The Font.—Carving on Bench-end.

Church of ST. GWITHIAN 136
    Engravings. View of Transept.—Plan of Oratory.—Doorway of same.—Remains of Porth Curnow Chapel.

	PAGE
Church of St. Ives	142

    Engravings. Shields from the Panels.—Section of Pier and Pier-arch moulding.—Chancel roof.—The Font.—Bench Standard.

Church of Towednack	148

    Engravings. General View.—Sections of Mouldings.—Plan of Tower Stairs.—Incised Stone.

Church of Zennor	151

    Engravings. Plan of Church.—Norman Window in Nave.—Window in Chancel.—Section and Hood-mould termination of same.

Church of St. Hilary	156

    Engravings. Blocked Spire-light.—General View of Tower, &c.

Church of St. Sithney	158
Church of St. Crowan	ib.
Church of Cramborne	ib.

    Engraving. Pulpit Panel.

General Notes upon the Western Cornish Churches.

Material	161
Ground-plans	162

    Engravings. General Plan of a Church.—View of Church of St. Gwinear.

Roodscreens	169
Towers	ib.

    Engravings. Pinnacle, Sancreed.—Pinnacle, St. Just.—Tower and Church of St. Mawgan in Meneage.—Turret, St. Burian.—Pinnacle, St. Mawgan.

Windows	173

    Engravings. General View of Church of S. Ruan Minor.—Various designs of Windows.—Window in Church of Gunwalloe.—From St. Mawgan.—From St. Erth.—From St. Just.—From St. Antony.

CONTENTS.	xi

PAGE

Roofs 177
Porches . . . . ib.
 Engravings. Porch of St. Burian.—Pinnacle, St. Mullion.
Mouldings and Sculpture . . . 179
 Engravings. Section of Pier, Sancreed.—Flower Ornament.—Impost, St Levan.—Impost, St. Sennen.—Impost, Sancreed.—Capital, Gunwalloe.—Cross, St. Ruan Major.—Stoup, Sancreed.
Names of the Patron Saints of Churches described in the Volume 183

Two Days in Cornwall with the Cambrian Archæological Association 187
 Engravings. Trembath Cross.—Boscawen-ûn Circle.—Plan of Barrow, near the same.—Stone found in the Barrow.—Urn found in the Barrow.—View of St. Sennen Church.—Section of Pier, St. Sennen Church.—Plan of Castle Treryn.—View of St. Levan's Church.—View of St. Burian's Church.—Carving from Roodscreen, St. Burian's Church.—Holed Stones, Bolleit.—The Pipers.—Plan of the Fogou.—Entrance to the Fogou.—Doorway, Trewoofe.—Plan of Hut, Chysauster.—Plan of Cave, Chapel-Uny.—Stone Amulet from same.—Plan of Beehive-hut, Bosphrennis.—Section of Masonry of same.—Exterior of Rectangular Chamber of same.—Entrance to Circular Chamber of the same.—Interior of Circular Chamber of the same.—Fallen Cromlech, Bosphrennis.—Plan of Hut, Bosullow.—Plan of Chûn Castle.—Masonry of Outer Wall of the same.—Chûn Cromlech.—Mên-an-tol, Madron.—Plan of St. Madron's Well.—Kistvaen, Samson, Scilly.

Index 237

CORNISH CHURCHES.

By J. T. Blight.

Illustrations by the Author.

I. THE DEANERY OF ST. BURIAN.

IN the latter part of the fifth and beginning of the sixth century, a numerous company of Irish saints—bishops, abbots, and sons and daughters of kings and noblemen—"came into Cornewaul and landed at Pendinas, a peninsula and stony rok, wher now the toun of St. Iës (St. Ives) standeth [a]." Hence they diffused themselves over the western part of the county, and at their several stations erected chapels and hermitages. Their object was to advance the Christian faith. In this they were successful, and so greatly were they reverenced, that whilst the memory of their holy lives still lingered in the minds of the people, churches were built on or near the sites of their chapels and oratories, and dedicated to Almighty God in their honour. Thus have their names been handed down to us. Few of them are mentioned in the calendars, or in the collections of the lives of saints, and what little is known of them has been chiefly derived from tradition. Dr. Whit-

[a] Leland.

aker believed that St. Burian, a king's daughter, was among those who landed at St. Ives, and that she took up her abode at the spot which now bears her name. Leland says,—

"St. Buriana, an holy woman of Ireland, sumtyme dwellid in this place, and there made an oratory. King Ethelstan, founder of St. Burian's College, and giver of the privileges and sanctuarie to it. King Ethelstan goyng hens, as it is said, on to Sylley, and returning, made, *ex voto*, a college where the oratorie was."

Whitaker gives full credit to the truth of this tradition :—

"Athelstan advanced towards the Land's End, in order to embark his army for the Sylley Isles. About four miles from it, but directly in the present road to it, as he was equally pious and brave, he went into an oratory, which had been erected there by an holy woman of the name of Burien, that came from Ireland, and was buried in her own chapel. Here he knelt down in prayer to God, full of his coming expedition against the Sylley Isles, and supplicating for success to it; then in a strain of devoutness that is little thought of now, but was very natural to a mind like his, at once munificent and religious, he vowed, if God blessed his expedition with success, to erect a college of clergy where the oratory stood, and to endow it with a large income. So, at least, says the tradition of St. Burien's itself no less than two centuries and a-half ago."

Having subdued the Scilly Isles, Athelstan on his return founded and endowed a collegiate church in honour of St. Buriana, on the spot called after her, Eglos-Berrie, about five miles eastward of the Land's End. "He gave lands and tithe of a considerable value for ever, himself becoming the first patron thereof, as his successors the Kings of England have been ever since." Athelstan also gave to the church the privileges of a sanctuary. The date of foundation is supposed to have been about the year 930. In Domesday Book reference is made to a college of canons here. The establishment consisted of a dean and three prebendaries, who are said to have held it from the king by the service of saying a hundred masses and a hundred psalters for the souls of the king and his ancestors. Dr. Whitaker alludes to a rector for the ruling church. Dr. Oliver says the clergy who first served the church were probably seven in number. Hals states that—

" The church or college consisted of Canons Augustines, or regular priests, and three prebendaries, who enjoyed the revenues thereof in common." He says that "about the time of Edward III., one of the popes obtruded upon this church, the canons and prebendaries thereof, a dean to be an inspector over them. This encroachment of the pope being observed by Edward, this usurpation was taken away."

From this statement it would be understood that the dean to whom reference is here made was the first who presided over the establishment, whereas we find it elsewhere recorded that this was the third dean, one John de Maunte, that he was objected to by the king on account of his being a foreigner, and that on this pretence Edward seized the establishment and kept it entirely in his own hands. It is also stated that, according to the foundation of Athelstan, the establishment was exempt from all inferior jurisdiction, there was no appeal from the local authorities but to the king himself. But Dr. Oliver, the highest authority on the subject, says " the foundation did not purport to confer any exemption from the jurisdiction of the ordinary, and, as far as documentary evidence can be traced, it is manifest that the diocesan exercised here the right of visitation as fully as in any other portion of the diocese." In his *Monasticon* will be found a *Vidimus* of the original endowment of this collegiate church by King Athelstan, on the 6th of October, 943,—"a date," says the Doctor, "evidently incorrect."

It appears that the establishment was well maintained for some time after the Conquest, but was subsequently much neglected from the non-residence of the deans. Leland wrote, " Their longeth to St. Buryens a deane and a few prebendarys, that almost be nether ther."

Much unpleasant feeling seems to have existed between the bishops of the diocese and the Crown respecting the control of this peculiar. Dr. Oliver tells us, that—

"On the death of Edmund, Earl of Cornwall, King Edward I. claiming St. Burian as a royal free chapel, gave Sir William de Hameldon, his chancellor, dean of York, and a great pluralist, this deanery of St. Burian. But the neglect of residence was properly objected to by Bishop Thomas Bitton, and a suit in the king's court was the consequence, which was not decided at the death of that prelate in 1307. His successor, Bishop Stapeldon, offered equal opposition when Queen Isabella appointed her chaplain, John Maunte, a foreigner, to this deanery."

Bishop Grandisson afterwards excommunicated this dean for "neglect of duty" and " disregard of his monitions." The dean's supporters within the parish of St. Burian were excommunicated with him :—

"On the 4th of November (1328), being at St. Michael's Mount, he (Bishop Grandisson) excommunicated with all form the principal delinquents, especially Richard Vivian, the most obnoxious of all. At his public visitation, on July 12, 1336, the bishop found the parishioners returned to a sense of duty, and truly repentant for their contumacy; and at their earnest supplication he absolved them from their censures, and preached to them from the text, 1 Peter ii. 25, 'Ye were as sheep going astray, but are now returned unto the shepherd and bishop of your souls.' To add to the Bishop's satisfaction, the dean, John de Maunte, on Aug. 16, 1336, waited upon him at Bishop's Court, Clyst, promised amendment in future, and took the oath of obedience to him and his successors in the see of Exeter.

"But the contest did not end here; within fifteen years King Edward III. revived the claim of exemption. But eventually the contest was terminated in favour of the stronger party, and to this day the dean receives institution from the Prince of Wales and Duke of Cornwall as his ordinary, though the patronage has often been exercised by the sovereign, *vacante ducatu* [b]."

The "church-town" of St. Burian stands on a high position, and the lofty tower is a very conspicuous object from the surrounding district. The spot commands extensive views, terminated on the south and west by the distant horizon of the Atlantic.

The church is a large building, consisting of a nave and north and south aisles, with a tower ninety feet in height at the west end. The dimensions of the building are about ninety feet by forty-seven. Not a vestige of the original church or college remains, for the present edifice was erected on the site of the older church in the fifteenth and sixteenth centuries. It is curious to observe that, though Polwhele in his History of Cornwall correctly refers this building to

[b] Oliver's *Monasticon*.

the fifteenth century, Dr. Whitaker in the supplement to the same work should be so mistaken as to describe it as the veritable church of Athelstan, erected more than eight centuries previously:—

"The inside," he says, "is still disposed nearly as Athelstan left it." And "its fresh appearance results merely from the frequent washings to which its high position on a hill and its pointed exposure to the rains from the Atlantic continually subject it."

Dr. Oliver gives in his *Monasticon* the act of the dedication of St. Burian's Church on the 26th of August, 1238, by Bishop Brewer of Exeter. But few relics even of the church of that period remain: the font may have stood there at that time, it is of Ludgvan granite[c], and has on the bowl three angels (not four as Dr. Oliver says) supporting shields; on a fourth shield is carved a plain Latin cross on two steps. On the opposite side there is a small Maltese cross between two of the angels. The height of the font is 2 ft. 11 in. It has been cleaned of the lime-wash which at one time covered it.

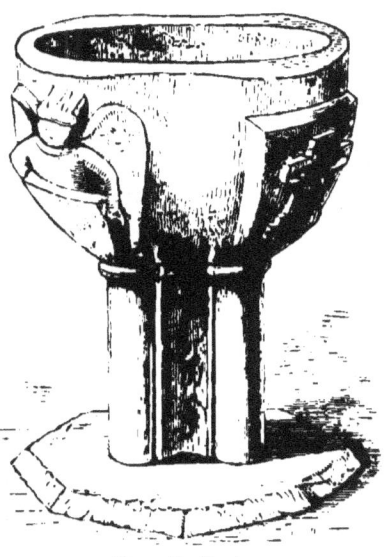

Font, St. Burian.

[c] The granite from Ludgvan parish is a better material for fine sculptured work than other granite found in the district.

In the early part of the present century this church was particularly rich in carved oak benches, and possessed a magnificent roodscreen and loft. In the year 1814 the building underwent repairs, when the benches and screen were barbarously destroyed. The plea for taking down the latter was, that it deadened the preacher's voice; a portion yet remains. About two-thirds of the curiously carved cornice has been placed in its original position, extending across south aisle and nave, and some of the beautiful arcade-work is preserved in a large chest within the church. The workmanship, as the accompanying cuts will shew, was exceedingly rich; the whole was gilded and painted, chiefly in red and blue, and each compartment was of a different design in the tracery. The screen extended the whole breadth of the church, and must have had a very fine effect. It was

Arcades of Roodscreen, St. Burian.

put together with wooden pins, no nails being used. The vandals who took it down do not appear to have had the least regard for it, for if they had no reverence for the holy things of the sanctuary, it would be thought that they would have taken some care to preserve the several portions merely for the sake of the beauty of the designs. Such, however, was not the case, for their saws were ruthlessly passed through the most elaborate tracery. It is said that some figures of saints belonging to this work were to be seen as chimney ornaments in the houses of the parishioners, and some of the bench-ends and panels were used as ordinary wood about farm out-houses.

On the upper part of the cornice is carved a vine pattern, beneath which are very curious scenes of hunting, warfare between animals and birds, and grinning heads: the workmanship is somewhat rude, but the effect is good. Some of the lower panels remain *in situ*, but no part of the connecting framework is to be found. The outer part of the screen was gilded and painted with different colours, red and blue predominating, but the inside, facing the altar, was entirely red. The spiral staircase, in the wall of the south aisle, which led to the rood-loft, has not been destroyed.

Adjoining the screen, within the chancel, are four oak miserere stalls, placed two on either side of the entrance from the nave to the chancel. Dr. Oliver says they were "destined for the dean, for the prebendary of Respernell, for the prebendary of Trithing, and for the holder of the 'Prebenda Parva.' Fortunately they have escaped destruction from the hands of the Puritans, and the no less mischievous pew-builders of more recent date." It has been suggested that when there was a choir at St. Burian's one of the stalls might have been for the precentor. Each stall has a moveable seat; when turned up, a rounded ledge is brought forward which served as a sort of occasional rest for the monks. The engraving shews one seat raised and the other down.

Misereres, St. Burian.

The chancel end of the church appears to have undergone alteration in modern times. The large east window, which has a pointed arch, does not retain its original tracery. A smaller square-headed window on the south side has been recently re-opened.

On the north side there was an unusual arrangement, which can now only be seen from the outside. Here we find that a large archway has been built up, and in connection with it immediately under the window of the north aisle there were three stone steps, evidently constructed with the original wall. These steps were to be seen about twenty or thirty years ago, and though now removed, their position may be traced.

There are no remains of a piscina either in the chancel or in the east end of the north or south aisle, for the church probably had three altars.

The aisles are connected with the nave by six pointed arches. The piers have a simple ogee moulding; the capitals, though of a plain character, have a bold effect. The aisles are each lighted by five square-headed windows, with hood-mouldings, divided into three lights, which are rounded at the top, and were inserted late in the sixteenth century.

The tower-arch is lofty, and its mouldings are bold and effective. Over the tower doorway, on the outside, is a shield bearing the sacred monogram I.H.S. The Perpendicular window above this is much supe-

Capital and Base of Pier, St. Burian.

rior to those at the east end of the church, and evidently of earlier date.

Within the tower, on the pavement, is an ancient tomb which, when Whitaker visited the church about sixty years ago, was "lying near the altar-rails, but on the floor in the northern access to it." According to Hals it was discovered about the year 1665, buried four feet in the ground, by the sexton while digging a grave. The inscription, he says, "was difficult to be read," but the "curious" found it to be " Jane, the wife of Geffery de Bolait, lies here: whosoever shall pray for her soul shall have five days pardon, M.I.X.IX." Another writer says, that "not only the year, but even the month and day of the month are both inserted," and he supposed it to mean "March 16, 1101." He then gives an incorrect reading of the inscription. At present there is no appearance of any date on the stone. The county histories vary in the wording of this inscription, owing probably to their authors inaccurately copying what had been previously published, and not taking the trouble to examine the monument for themselves.

As will be seen from the engraving on the next page, the inscription, which is in Norman-French, is cut in letters of the thirteenth century, and runs as follows :—✠ CLARICE : LA : FEMME : CHEFFREI : DE : BOLLEIT : GIT : ICI : DEV : DE : LALME : EIT : MERCE : KE : PVR : LEALME : PVNT (PRIUNT) : DI : IOR : DE : PARDVN : AVERVND—" ✠ Clarice the wife of Geoffry de Bolleit lies here, God of her soul have mercy : who pray for her soul shall have ten days pardon." The stone is seven feet long, and has a floriated cross on three steps carved in relief on the upper part. The family of Bolleit resided on an estate of the same name in this parish.

The tower, which is constructed entirely of wrought granite, is divided into four stages, and has double buttresses at each angle. The newel staircase is contained in an octagonal turret which rises picturesquely above the parapets at the south-east corner.

The bells are three in number. The largest has this legend, "Virginis egre-

Tomb of Clarice de Bolleit, St. Burian.

giæ vocor campana Mariæ," i.e. "I am called the Bell of the glorious Virgin Mary;" and the date 1738. It is singular to find such a legend on a post-Reformation bell; probably, however, it was in that year recast and the original legend reproduced. The bell has a flaw or crack running through it, for which the following tradition accounts. The bell was cast in the village of St. Burian, and before it had hardened, a man jumped from a hedge near the mould, which being disturbed by the shake, rendered the bell imperfect. Its diameter is 3 ft. 9 in., an unusually large size for Cornish bells. The next bell has for its legend, " Vocem ego do vobis: vos date verba Deo," i.e. "I give to you a voice; give ye words to God." Date 1638, diameter 3 ft. 6 in. The third bell has the names of the Churchwardens,—" Mr. Richard Davies, Sampson Hutchens—wardens, 1681." Diameter 3 ft.

The porch is surmounted with battlements, has double buttresses at the angles finished with crocketed pinnacles, and a bold stringcourse. Within are stone benches on either side, and a mutilated stoup. Over the church door is a bracket, on which may have been placed an image of the Blessed Virgin, or of St. Burian, the patron saint of the church.

When Bishop Stapeldon visited St. Burian, in 1314, he took the following inventory of the church property :—

"Three suits entire of vestments with tunics and dalmatics; two copes for the choir; two chalices; one good missal, and another inferior; one antiphonar, with a middling good psaltery (*psalterium in medio bonum*); two grails in excellent condition ; a trophar ; a legend, and one old antiphonar ; a veil for Lent ; nine towels ; a nuptial veil ; a pall for the dead ; three pair of corporals ; and three surplices[d]."

Near the porch, on the right hand side of the path, is an ancient cross on a flight of five steps. Another cross stands without the churchyard, and there is a tradition that the churchyard at one time surrounded it. This, however, is not probable.

About a mile south-east of St. Burian, on the estate of Bosliven, are some remains of an ancient building, to this day called "the sanctuary." It has been considered as the original "sanctuary" of Athelstan, but the title and privileges of sanctuary pertained to the church, the churchyard, and sometimes a limited space beyond. C. S. Gilbert says of these ruins that they appear to be the remains of the chapel attached to the Deanery-house. Dr. Oliver mentions a "capella Sancti Silvani" as having existed in this parish. The building at Bosliven appears to have been much larger than the other ancient chapels of which remains are found throughout Cornwall. But whatever it may have been, sanctuary, chapel, or oratory, it seems to have incited the rage of the Puritans; for it was almost totally destroyed by Shrubsall, one of Cromwell's miserable instruments of sacrilege. This fact alone is sufficient proof that at that time it was a sacred edifice of some note.

The adjacent parishes of St. Levan and St. Sennen form part of the deanery of St. Burian.

[d] Oliver's *Monasticon*.

ST. LEVAN Church, about three miles s.w. from St. Burian, is situated in a most romantic spot, in a deep hollow, scarcely a furlong from the cliffs. The celebrated Logan Rock is in the immediate neighbourhood, and the adjoining coast is acknowledged to rank among the finest coast-scenery in England. So abrupt is the hollow (or "gulph," as a Cornish historian expresses it) in which the church stands, that the four pinnacles of the tower are all that can be seen of the building for any considerable distance when approaching it from the east or west.

The church consists of a nave, south aisle and north transept, a tower at the west end, and a small porch. The aisle is lighted on the south by three square-headed windows with hood-mouldings, and has pointed windows at the east and west ends. The arch of the chancel-window is more obtuse than that at the east end of the aisle; both have been partially built up from the sill and filled with wooden frames. The arched window at the north end of the transept has also been despoiled of its stone tracery. In the west side of this transept is a small lancet-window. Some of the quoins of the jambs of this window are of sandstone, a material easily worked, but not the best that might have been chosen in such a locality. It must have been brought from the neighbourhood of Hayle, where the sand on the shore is in some places becoming changed into solid rock. An account of this curious formation, by Dr. Paris, will be found in the "Transactions of the Geological Society of Cornwall," and in his "Guide to the Mount's Bay." Some of this stone may also be found in the wall near the east window of the north aisle at St. Burian's.

An arched doorway in the angle between the nave and the transept has been walled up. A square-headed window near it has had its mullions taken away, and is filled with a wooden frame. The arch of the tower doorway consists of two plain cavetto mouldings, under a hoodmould.

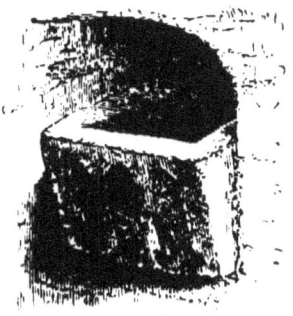

Stoup, St. Levan.

Entering by the porch, the first object to be noticed is the stoup, which is perfect. It is square, and ornamented with simple arcading on one side. Adjoining the doorway is a carved representation of two jesters. The floor of the church is two steps below the doorway.

Internally the building is in a most dilapidated and neglected state, extremely damp, and with the atmosphere of a vault. The walls and arcades have been from time to time liberally coated with lime-wash, and modern pews have been introduced to break the uniformity of the original benches. Some of the panels of the roodscreen remain, and have curiously carved shields. On one are represented the figures of a winged bullock, a winged cat or lion, and two human heads with the heads and wings of birds above them, (one of the birds has also the head of another animal projecting from the hinder part of its neck,) and the legs and feet of some quadruped.

Bench-ends, St. Levan.

These may have reference to the vision of Ezekiel or to the mystical beasts described in the Revelation of St. John. On other shields are devices symbolical of the Passion, as the spear, the nails, the hammer, and the cross, encircled with the crown of thorns. But the intruding pews hide much of the work. Some of the bench-ends are also curiously carved. One has a pilgrim monk with a breviary and a discipline. The illustrations will give a general idea of the rest. One

Monogram, St. Levan.

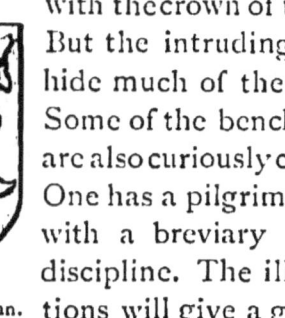

Bench-end, St. Levan.

female has a sort of network over the hair not unlike that worn at the present time. The sacred monogram I.H.S. is repeated in a variety of forms. There are

West View of Transept, St. Levan.

other monograms probably intended to be commemorative of forgotten benefactors of the church: a good

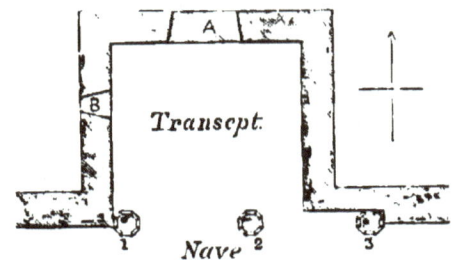

Plan of Transept.
A. B. mark the position of Windows ; 1. 2. 3. Piers.

example is given on p. 17. There are many other carvings suggestive of sacred subjects. The nave and aisle are connected by an arcade of six low, pointed arches. The piers of these arches are octagonal, and the capitals consist merely of rounded and hollow mouldings. The oldest and most interesting part of the church is the transept, which is evidently Early English, and was probably erected early in the thirteenth

Interior of Transept, St. Levan.

century. The high-pitched roof, lancet window, and other details are characteristic of the style of that period. Each side of the arch of this little window, which is about 3 ft. 3 in. high, is formed of one stone

Capital of Pier (2).

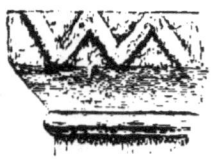

Capital of Pier (3).

with a chamfered edge. The modern wooden frame is omitted in the opposite engraving. The transept and nave are connected by two arches with octagonal piers, but the capitals differ from those of the aisle-piers. The middle one, which has sustained some injury, is curiously chamfered at each angle. The eastern pier (3 in plan) is almost entirely hidden by the pulpit; a part of the capital is, however, exposed to view: it is ornamented with the zigzag moulding, and has the appearance of being Norman,—the relic, perhaps, of an older church. The roof of the transept has been entirely plastered. The font appears to be transitional from Norman to Early English. About twenty years ago it was carefully scraped and cleaned — it is therefore free from lime-wash, and its star and cable mouldings are in good preservation. The height of the font is 2 ft. 6 in., and the diameter of the bowl is 2 ft. It has no base or step.

Font, St. Levan.

The wood-work of the roofs of the nave and aisle is handsomely carved, and was originally painted and gilt. Some traces of this decoration may still be seen.

The tower has a rude round-headed arch springing from pentagonal imposts. It contains two bells, which have no legends. One has the date 1641; the other has the names of the churchwardens and the founder's mark,—a bell with the initials A. R.

In the churchyard are two ancient crosses: the taller one, nearly seven feet high, stands near the porch, and is a good example of its class.

Dr. Oliver is of opinion that the patron saint of this church is St. Livin, an Irish bishop, who preached the Gospel in Belgium, and suffered martyrdom A.D. 656.

The well and chapel of St. Levan stood on the edge of the cliff, a little below the church. Some remains of the well may yet be seen. There are also the ruins of the four walls of an ancient chapel at Porth-curnow, about half a mile distant.

The descriptions of churches, where any are given, in the county histories, are extremely meagre. C. S. Gilbert's is probably the best general history of Cornwall, yet all he can say of the interesting little church of St. Levan is, that it contains carved shields bearing the arms of Vyvyan and Trethurffe, and "a curious figure of the devil."

The church of ST. SENNEN, or Senanus, an Irish abbot who accompanied St. Burian into Cornwall, is four miles from St. Levan, and rather more than that distance from St. Burian. It is a small, low structure, standing on high ground about a mile from the Land's End, and exposed to all the storms of the Atlantic. The plan of this church is nearly the same as that of St. Levan; here, however, the chancel projects beyond the aisle, which is not the case at St. Levan. The aisle has three arched windows on the south side, and one at either end. The chancel window has a round head. A square-headed window with a hood-moulding, on the south side of the chancel, is blocked up. The transept has two windows, one square-headed, the other arched. The flat-headed north doorway is also walled up. The stone mullions and tracery of all the windows have been removed, and their places occupied by ugly wooden frames. The belfry-lights alone remain in their original condition. Internally the church is in a most dilapidated condition, and, like its neighbour, has been plentifully bedaubed with lime-wash. An arcade of six arches connects the nave and aisle. The piers are shafted at the angles, the capitals consisting simply of round and cavetto mouldings. The transept is connected with the nave by a single four-centred arch.

Capital, St. Sennen.

The roodscreen has been entirely destroyed. The font has a modern appearance, but stands on an ancient base, which has an inscription in Old English letters. Hals, who visited the church in 1700, writes—

"The sexton shewed me an inscription on the foot of the font-stone, which he told me several bishops of Exeter and their priests, in their triennial visitations at Buryan and this church, had viewed and inspected, but could not read it. Whereupon, in like manner, I observed on the font-stone the said inscription in a barbarous strange character of letters, of which 1 could see but part, by reason of a new pew or seat which was built on a part of it: however, I interpreted that which I saw to consist of these letters,—Anno Dom. mille. cccc xx. or xl.; in the year of our Lord 1420 or 1440. Let the curious remove the seat and explain the rest; probably the church was then erected."

The stone has been removed to its present position since Hals saw it, and is not now hidden by any pew. The inscription is of the fifteenth century, in the letters and with the usual abbreviations of the period. A portion of it has been broken away; the remainder appears to be as follows:—" Eccla ī decote S. I. B. dedica fvit anno dni millo CCCCXLI.:" in full, "[Hæc] Ecclesia in decollatione Sancti Johannis Baptistæ dedicata fuit, Anno Domini Millesimo quadringentesimo quadragesimo primo," (*secundo, tertio,* or *quarto,* as the case may have been; for a portion of the date has evidently been broken away with the missing fragment); and in English, "This church was dedicated on the festival of the beheading of St. John the Baptist, A.D. 1441-4." Hals also tells us that the sexton shewed him "the headless bodies of some images of human shape cut in alabaster that were not long before found hid in the walls of the same, all curiously wrought, which also had been painted with gold, vermilion, and blue bice, on several parts of their garments." One of these images still remains, standing on a bracket which projects from the north wall of the transept. It is 3 ft. 2 in. high. Repeated coats of lime have entirely covered all "gold, vermilion, and blue bice." And the figure has received rough usage; the head and arms are gone. It was probably mutilated by the Puritans, perhaps by Shrubsall himself, fresh from the demolition of the sanctuary. This image represents a female saint, most probably the Blessed Virgin.

The tower has two bells: one lies on the belfry-floor; it was cast by Thomas Bayley of Bridgewater, in the year 1762: the other bell was cast in 1810.

Mutilated Image of the Blessed Virgin, St. Sennen.

II. ST. MADRON—ST. PAUL—SANCREED—ST. JUST.

Among the many traditions of Cornwall none are more popular than those which tell of the marvellous strength of the ancient inhabitants of the county. The peculiar forms and positions of huge rocks, and the numerous rude and Cyclopean structures, are generally considered good evidence of the existence of a giant race. In like manner are marvellous tales told of the selection of sites for churches and of their erection. For instance, it is said that when a church was finished, its patron saint stood on the tower, and taking the builder's hammer, swung it around his head and let it take what direction it might. Wherever it fell, there was the next church to be erected.

The hammer thrown for St. MADRON fell on a

pleasant place. The church stands on the brow of an eminence which slopes gradually down for about two miles to the shores of Mount's Bay. The famed St. Michael's Mount itself is seen distinctly, and beyond it the long cloud-like coast which terminates with the Lizard Point.

It is recorded that in the time of Richard I., Henry de Pomeraye (or Pomeroi—the word is spelt in a variety of ways) built or endowed the church of St. Madron, and gave it to the Knights Hospitallers of St. John of Jerusalem, for the health and salvation of his own soul, that of his lord the King, and the souls of his father, mother, brother, sisters, progenitors, and successors. Among the entries relating to the English houses of the Hospitallers in Dugdale's *Monasticon* is the following:—" Trebigh Præceptoria. Henricus de Pomeria dedit Hospitalariis Ecclesiam S. Maderi, cum pertinentiis, in com. Cornubiæ, pertinentem eidem præceptoriæ." The Knights Hospitallers are said to have had a provincial establishment at Landithy, an estate immediately adjoining the church. This church is called "Ecclesia de Sancti Madderni" in the Taxation of Pope Nicholas, A.D. 1291.

Of the church which Henry de Pomeroi built or endowed nothing remains excepting the font, which is Norman. The lead with which it is lined is brought over the upper edge and nearly half-way down the side. The forms of square panels may be seen on one side,—doubtless the other sides were similar;

but the font appears to have received violent injury; portions have been plastered up, and it is also thickly coated with lime. The block of granite on which it

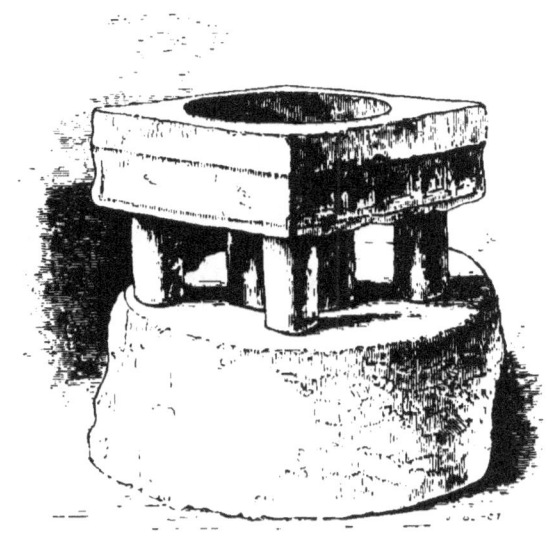

Font, St. Madron.

stands is extremely rude. The dimensions of the font are as follow:—Height, 3 ft. 5 in.; height of shafts, 11 in.; length of each side, 2 ft. 6 in.

The present church consists of a nave and chancel, with north and south aisles, and a tower at the west end of the nave. The two lower stages of the tower and the east end of the chancel (the ancient sanctuary) are much older than any other portions of the building, and form parts of the church which was rebuilt on the site of Pomeroi's church in the beginning of the fourteenth century. The south aisle was, perhaps, built early in the fifteenth century, along the nave only, and extended along the chancel at a subsequent period. The north aisle is later. In the south wall of the sanctuary are a sedile and piscina

Sedile and Piscina, St. Madron.

under a single hoodmould. There were probably three sedilia; for, though only one remains, the springing of a second arch may still be seen, extending westward to the end of the wall, which has been cut away to make room for the late arcades. The height of the sedile is 4 ft. 7 in.; the breadth 3 ft. The registers of the see state that Bishop Grandisson consecrated the high-altar on the 13th of July, 1336. Apart from this direct evidence, it would not have been unreasonable to have fixed from 1320 to 1340 for the date of the sedile and piscina. There is a niche near the east end of the south wall in the south aisle which looks very like a piscina, but there is no drain. There is a smaller niche, similarly placed, in the north aisle,—perhaps an ambrie. Both are of late character. The east window is modern, and not in good taste; it is of two lights, transomed, and filled with stained glass; as are also the windows in the east and west ends of the aisles. There are also three coloured windows in the side of the south aisle, and one in the side of the north aisle, which was given by the ladies of the parish. The window in the east end of the south aisle contains the arms of its donors, some of the principal families of the parish,—Borlase, Peters, Tremenheere, Le Grice, and Scobell. One of the windows in the side of the south aisle is commemorative of the late Major-General Robyns. The best window of the whole, as regards the quality of the glass, is that in the west end of the north aisle: it is the gift of the present vicar and patron, the Rev. M. N. Peters.

The aisles open into the nave by an arcade of six four-centred arches on either side. The piers on the south side of the nave are composed of four three-quarter round shafts, with a hollow moulding between each. The capitals are good, with simple mouldings. The piers on the north side of the nave are of a different character; their mouldings are the same as those in St. Just Church, of which engravings will be given hereafter: the capitals are ornamented with foliage.

Some fragments of the roodscreen remain, and on one of the pew-doors, evidently not their original position, are carved the arms of Henry VIII.; this carving is probably of the same date as the north aisle. A description of these arms, with an accurate engraving, may be seen in the GENTLEMAN'S MAGAZINE for May, 1842.

Window of Second Stage of Tower, St. Madron.

The tower is probably contemporaneous with the fourteenth-century work at the east end, with the exception of the uppermost stage, which was added at a subsequent period. It is plain, without buttresses, and is very substantially built, the walls being four

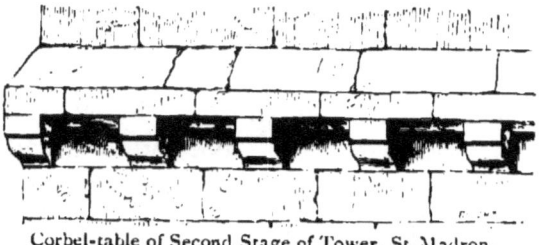

Corbel-table of Second Stage of Tower, St. Madron.

feet in thickness. Externally the junction between the older walls and the aisles is apparent. The tower-arch is a perfectly plain soffit-arch of masonry. The doorway has simply a chamfer. The window over it is a modern restoration, filled with stained glass. On the north side is a square turret, reaching to the second stage, and containing a newel staircase. The corbel-table below the uppermost stage is very good and effective.

Loosely placed in the piscina are some remarkable alabaster figures of archangels, very excellently sculptured. They stood in rows, one above the other, and each holds a spear in the right hand and a reversed shield in the left. They are entirely gilded excepting the inner parts of the wings, which are coloured red and blue in each alternate figure. These fragments may have belonged to some tomb, or probably to an ancient reredos. The height of the fragment represented by the accompanying cut is ten inches.

Figures of Archangels, St. Madron.

There are several mural monuments in the church. One, date 1631, is inscribed with "an Epitaphe to y^e memorye of y^e deceased Thomas Fleming, Gent." This family once held considerable property in the parish. There is also a monumental brass on the wall of the north aisle.

In the churchyard is the oft-quoted epitaph on George Daniel:—

> "Belgia me Birth, Britain me Breeding gave,
> Cornwall a Wife, ten children and a grave"

These lines are on a newly-cut stone, the original inscription having been almost obliterated.

The parish registers commence with the year 1577. In the baptismal register for 1594 reference is made to the "daughter of George the Miller;"—" a curious fragment," says Mr. Halliwell, "in the history of the origin of English surnames."

St. Madron Church has not been allowed to fall into a state of decay for want of timely repairs.

ST. PAUL.—This church stands on the summit of a hill overlooking the fishing village of Mousehole, and is about three miles from Penzance. It possesses few architectural features of interest, for it is perhaps the most sadly disfigured church in the west of Cornwall. Some historical interest is, however, attached to the spot; for in the year 1595 the Spaniards paid a hostile visit to this parish, and, says Carew,—

> "Burned not onely the houses they went by, but also the parish church of *Paul*, the force of the fire being such, as it vtterly ruined all the great stonie pillers thereof; others of them in that time burned that fisher towne Mowsehole; the rest marched as a gard for defence of these firers."

In reference to this subject the parish register thus commences:—

"Jesu spes et Salus mea.
"1595.

"A register of the names of all those that were baptised, married, and buried in the Parish Church of St. Pawle in the Countie of Cornwall, from the 23rd Daie Julie, the year of our Lord God 1595, on the which Daie the Church, towre, bells, and all other things pertaining to the same, together with the houses and goods, was Burn'd and spoil'd by the Spaniards in the said parish, being Wensdaie the daie aforsaid, in the 37th yeare of the Reigne of our Sovereigne Ladie Elizabeth, by the grace of God, of England, Fraunce, and Ireland, defender of the Faith.

"Per me JOHANNEM TREMEARNE, Vicarium Ejus."

If the stonework of the tower was injured, it was evidently restored with the original materials; but the greater probability is, that only the woodwork was destroyed, which of course involved the destruction of the bells. The tower was erected perhaps about the end of the fifteenth century. There is a tradition in the parish to the effect that the Spaniards met some of the country people bearing fagots of furze, and driving them into the church compelled them to drop their bundles, to which they set fire; and as it happened to be a strong southwest wind, they opened wide the door to receive the benefit of its aid. When the porch was opened for repairs, in the year 1807, some of the woodwork was found to be charred. This fact supports other evidence that the church was not totally demolished. Nearly all the timber in it was probably consumed, and doubtless some portions of the walls suffered much; but Carew's statement, that "all the great stonie pillers" were "vtterly ruined" requires some qualification,— for the present piers, though they might subsequently have undergone repair, were evidently constructed previous to the landing of the Spaniards. The arches appear to have been clumsily repaired, for they incline a little to the north and south of the nave, and to prevent them from falling they are connected by unseemly iron braces bolted through the spandrels. The south doorway and the western part of the wall, including the doorway of the north aisle, also escaped destruction. It therefore appears that the building was simply gutted, and that the walls at the eastern end only were so much injured as to require to be rebuilt. Although at the time the Spaniards left it, it could not have been in a fit condition for the usual public worship, yet the services of baptism, marriage, and burial were undoubtedly celebrated within the walls : for the Vicar says in the register, "*From* the 23rd daie of Julie," &c.,—which implies that it was still possible to perform these necessary services within the church. The destruction by fire, in the year 1853, of the neighbouring parish church of St. Hilary, affords a melancholy instance of the amount of injury a building of like description would incur under similar circumstances. This church, however, probably received more damage than that of St. Paul, yet whilst it was still unroofed and blackened by the effects of fire a marriage was celebrated at its altar.

The present church of St. Paul is of large dimensions. The nave and aisles are connected by nine four-centred arches, but the third arch westward from the chancel on the north side of the nave is of peculiar formation. As will be seen by reference

Arch between Nave and North Aisle, St. Paul.

to the accompanying cut it is very small, and is constructed on a solid block of masonry, which is 3 ft. 6 in. above the floor. This arch may have been in some way connected with the rood-loft and screen, or perhaps it was a hagioscope from the transept which the aisle replaced. It is of earlier date than any other part of the building except the tower.

The windows of the aisles are of churchwarden insertion, ugly and round-headed; and the east window is a perfect caricature. All have wooden frames with large panes of glass.

The tower, like all church-towers in the western part of Cornwall, is constructed entirely of wrought granite. It is a fine building, divided into three stages, with double buttresses at the angles. The newel staircase, like that at St. Burian, is contained in a turret which rises above the embattled parapet. The mullions and tracery have been removed from the large tower-window, which is filled up in the most barbarous manner. Over this window and on either side is a niche, from which the ancient images have been removed. On the lower part of the niche on the left of the window is carved the letter M, which, of course, indicates that the image of the Blessed Virgin stood here; the niche on the other side has a blank shield. The hoodmoulding over the doorway springs from two corbel-heads, and at the centre of the mould is a shield bearing the sacred characters I. H. C. The belfry-lights retain their original tracery, which is very good of its kind. The tower-arch is of very excellent proportions; it is su-

Tower, St. Paul.

perior to those in most other churches in this district. The three bells are each dated 1727, with the initials A. R., and have the following legends:— North bell (diameter, 2 ft. 10 in.), "Prosperity to this parish;" middle bell (diameter, 3 ft. 3 in.), "Prosperity to the Church of England;" south bell (diameter, 3 ft. 3 in.), "To the church the living call: To the grave do summon all."

Belfry Windows, St. Paul.

There is a mural monument, dated 1689, in the north aisle, to William Godolphin, of Trewarveneth, in this parish: he is said to have been the last representative of that ancient and noble family. Two swords and pieces of armour are hung over the stone. There is also a most elaborate monument here, to the memory of "Stephen Hutchens of this parish, who departed this life at Port Royall in Jamaica, the 24th day of August, 1709:"—

"He hath given one hundred pounds towards the repairing and beautifying this church, and six hundred pounds for building a house for six poor men and six poor women born in this parish."

We are also informed by a quotation from, or rather variation of, the 112th Psalm, that Stephen Hutchens "saw his desire upon his enemies." The monument is in the most florid style: there are representations of shattered vessels, warlike instruments and trophies, with a profile likeness of Queen Anne. It is worthy of notice only because it bears an old Cornish inscription :—

> "Bounas heb dueth Eu poes Karens wei
> tha Pobl Bohodzhak Paull han Egles nei."

Which has been rendered into English thus :—

> "Eternal life be his whose loving care
> Gave Paul an alms-house and the church repair."

It was the custom at one time to place Cornish inscriptions in churches, but this appears to be the only one now remaining.

Particular interest is attached to this church on account of its being the burial-place of Dolly Pentreath, said to have been the last person able to converse in the old Cornish language. A well-cut granite obelisk has lately been erected here in commemoration of this tradition. The monument is inscribed with the name of Dorothy Pentreath, which was the maiden name of the old woman, for it appears that she was married to a person of the name of Jeffery. This, however, is of no great importance, for she is popularly known as Dolly Pentreath, and it is still the custom in the villages of Mousehole and Newlyn for women to be called by their maiden names after marriage; indeed, there are some instances in which the husband goes by the maiden name of his wife, she being the more popular or more important personage of the two.

This church was attached to the mitred abbey of

Hailes, in Gloucestershire, and is dedicated to St. Paulinus, first Archbishop of York, who was sent into England by Pope Gregory soon after the mission of St. Augustine. In the Taxation of Pope Nicholas, A.D. 1291, it is entered as "Ecclesia Sancti Paulini."

Should any reader of this paper visit the church of St. Paul let him not forget to ascend to the roof of the tower: the magnificent view from the summit is well worthy of the labour.

SANCREED Church lies in a secluded spot among the hills about three miles westward from Penzance.

That there was a church here at the end of the thirteenth century is proved by the Taxation of Pope Nicholas IV., where it occurs as "Ecclesia Sancti Sancredi." There are probably no existing remains of this building, except perhaps in the foundations and the lower parts of the walls of the present church, which appears to have been erected late in the fifteenth century. Its plan nearly resembles that of St. Levan—consisting of a nave and a south aisle, a south porch, a north transept, and a low tower at the west end of the nave: the walls of the tower are very massive. The font is similar to that at St. Burian; it has four angels, with crosses on their foreheads, and bearing shields. The stoup remains, and there is a niche for an image over the south door. The roodscreen has been removed, but some of its curiously-carved panels are preserved in the vestry at the north end of the transept. These panels consist of two large pieces of woodwork, 8 ft. 6 in.

Panels of Roodscreen, Sancreed.

and 8 ft. 4 in. respectively in length, the panels following in succession as they were originally placed. The carved figures are undoubtedly symbolical, though some seem more than usually grotesque. The crowned head with three faces, represented in the annexed cut, is of course intended to symbolize the Holy Trinity. The trellis-like pattern on this panel is the same as that on the Norman font at

Green's Norton, Northamptonshire (see Simpson's Baptismal Fonts). The eagle on the third panel is very spirited. In the first panel is a spotted goat devouring the tender branches of the vine. Others contain—an owl, two-headed female figures, serpents entwined, a crowned serpent, and the pelican. These carvings were richly painted, like those of the screen at St. Burian.

The windows, with the exception of the belfry-lights, have been treated in the usual barbarous manner.

In the churchyard is a tall round-headed cross, on which is cut, among other devices, a representation of the lily of the Blessed Virgin,—a symbol very frequently used during the fifteenth century. There is another ancient cross by the west gate.

ST. JUST IN PENWITH [e].—The church-town of St. Just is situated on the coast, in a wild and romantic spot between the Land's End and the parish of Morvah.

Bishop Grandisson dedicated the high-altar of a church at this place on the 13th of July, 1336,—the same day with St. Madron; but nothing now remains of that church, for the east end of the chancel, which was the only portion of it that remained at that time, was taken down to be rebuilt in the year 1834. The rest of the church was erected late in the fifteenth century, and it is of nearly the same plan as St. Burian. The porch is the same as St. Burian's,

[e] So called to distinguish it from St. Just in Roseland.

Cornish Churches. 41

excepting that there is a stairway from the interior of the church leading to its roof: the doorway to this is now walled up. The interior of the church presents rather a singular appearance, owing to the pier-arches being of different breadths,—some being pointed, and some depressed and nearly semicircular. The capitals of the piers are richly sculptured with foliage,—a very frequent design being that of leaves bound with their twisted stems as with cords. The same may be seen at St. Madron, and the mouldings of the St. Just piers correspond to those of the north (or later) aisle at St. Madron. Some of the capitals have angels bearing shields, on which are carved the arms of several of the principal families connected with the parish, and which were probably benefactors to the church.

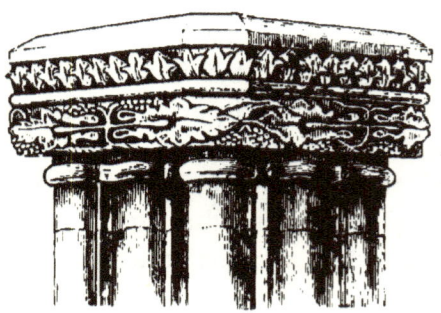

Capital, St. Just.

Capital, St. Just.

The capital of the second pier westward from the chancel has an angel with a shield, on which are the letters M. J., for MARIA JESUS. The hoodmould-terminations of one of the south aisle windows bear the same letters, but in reversed order, and are noticeable for their singular design. In writing on these letters, in his "Account of St. Just," Mr. Buller, a late vicar, seems to have overlooked evidence which would have supported his interpretation, had there been any doubt as to the letters themselves; for around the J are five bosses, and around the M seven; the former, as is well known, being symbolical of the five wounds in the body of our Lord, and the latter the seven dolours of the Blessed Virgin. The round-headed termination of the J, with the two similar forms on its upper part, may represent the three nails; for in the arms of the Passion three nails were sometimes used instead of four.

Hoodmould, St. Just.

The last capital westward on the north side of the nave has a curious variety of the tooth-moulding.

Tooth-moulding, St. Just.

The aisles have each five pointed windows, with tracery of two patterns, which alternate in each aisle. The east windows of the aisles are very singular. They are alike, having four lights, with depressed heads above filled with Perpendicular tracery of flamboyant character. The east window is a recent imitation of one of the side windows of the aisles. The tower is of a plain character, with embattled parapet and four pinnacles, but no buttresses. It diminishes toward the top too abruptly for its height to have a pleasing effect. There are three bells, two of which have legends. On one, "Sancte Michael, ora pro nobis:" on the other, "Protege Virgo pia Quos convoco, Sancta Maria."

When the old sacrarium was taken down in 1834, there was found in the wall an inscribed stone, bear-

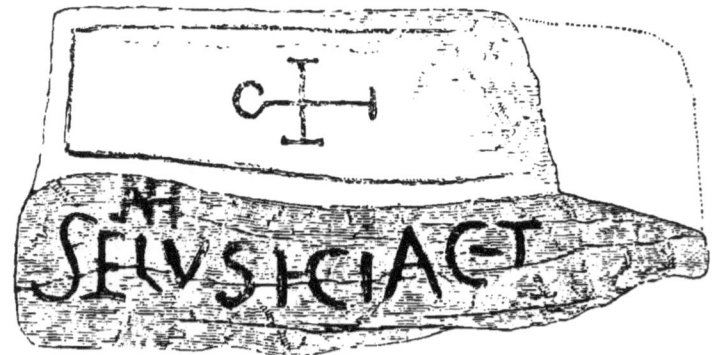

Inscribed Stone, St. Just.

ing on one side the words "Silus [or Selus] hic jacet." There are also some marks over the first word which look very like a monogram. On the upper side of the stone, as it is now placed, is an incised cruciform pastoral-staff, indicating that the monument was commemorative of an ecclesiastic of some authority. In the same walls were found the broken parts of a piscina and the capital of a pier of Norman date.

III. CURY—GUNWALLOE—MULLION.

THE district of Meneage measures about ten miles, from its northern boundary to its termination at the Lizard Point—the southernmost land of England; and its greatest breadth from east to west—that is, from sea to sea—does not exceed ten miles. Within this small compass there are no fewer than twelve parish churches. Some of these are situated in secluded spots, embosomed in rich foliage; whilst others stand on open and exposed situations on the table-land. One, Gunwalloe, on the very margin of the sea, is often dashed by the foam in stormy weather.

Various are the interpretations given to the word Meneage, such as *menég*, 'stony;' *mean-ake*, 'the deaf stone;' *mencog*, 'kept in by the sea:' it is also said to mean the 'heath-stone,' from the fact of the beautiful Cornish heath, *Erica vagans*, growing plentifully over the serpentine rock of the district. "Menege," says Norden, "is a parcell of lande contayning the most part of this Kirrier hundred; a fruteful and plentifull place for people, corne, fleshe, fishe, tynn, and copper." This reference to tin and copper is not correct,—at least the district is not now disfigured by unsightly mine works; it is almost wholly an agricultural country. One side of Mount's Bay is formed by its western coast. The headlands, coves, and arched rocks along this shore are of the most varied and beautiful description; the peculiar character of the serpentine rock giving to the cliffs greater brilliancy of colour, though they have not the same savage grandeur as those at the Land's End.

When the wild downs in this tract of land were dense forests, through which wild beasts prowled, and about that period when the inhabitants began to change their Celtic religion for a purer faith, then, says tradition, saints came from afar, and here made their abodes in little hermitages. Of these were St. Rumon and St. Corantyne, afterwards Bishops of Cornwall. "St. Corantyne," says Dr. Borlase, "who is now called Cury, was the first Cornish apostle of note that we know of. He was consecrated Bishop of Cornwall by St. Martin, Bishop of Tours in France, and, being said to have converted all Cornwall, died in the year 401." Dr. Whitaker, however, who appears to have taken considerable pains to controvert Dr. Borlase on all points, states that St. Corantyne "certainly died in a much earlier year."

In the Domesday Book Cury was taxed under the jurisdiction of Buchent, now Bochym, a barton in the parish, and at that time of some note. In the reign of Henry VI. we find it called Curytowne. In Wolsey's Inquisition it is entered as Curyton, and was then presented with Breage, Germoe, and Gunwalloe as one living, Breage being the mother church.

The church of ST. CURY (or Corantyne) is about one mile from the sea, and consists of a chancel, nave, south transept, north aisle, a tower at the west end of the nave, and a small porch. Originally it

South Doorway, Cury.

was undoubtedly cruciform. The south doorway, probably the sole relic of an earlier church, is in the

Norman style, perhaps of the latter part of the eleventh or beginning of the twelfth century.

The nave, chancel, and transept appear to have been erected at the end of the fourteenth century; but the window in the transept is modern, as is also the chancel window.

The aisle, of fifteenth-century character, is connected with the nave by six four-centred arches. The piers are shafted at the angles, the space between each being a plain cavetto mould. The capitals are ornamented with a simple and angular kind of foliage. The east window of this aisle is the largest in the building, and has four lights with geometrical tracery; the splay of the arch internally is filled with quatrefoil ornamentation—a very rare feature.

Hagioscope.

At the junction of the chancel and transept a remarkable hagioscope is formed by a large chamfer of the angle, supported by a detached shaft and arches to small responds of similar character. Externally the wall has been thickened out into two

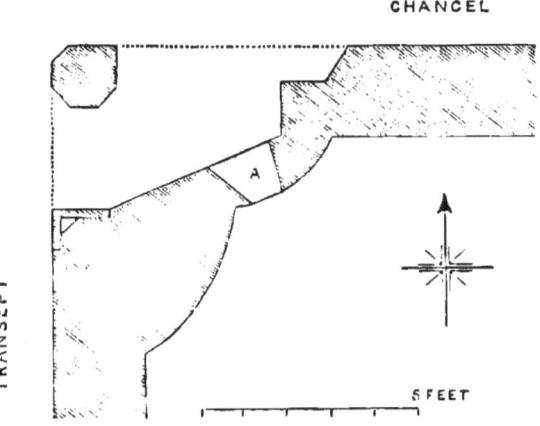

Plan of Hagioscope, Cury. A. Low Side Window.

rounded projections, on the inner side of the smaller of which is a window (see opposite cut), which may have been used as a "low side window;" within, it is four feet seven inches above the floor, and its dimensions are 1 ft. 4 in. high by 9 in. wide. A similar arrangement is found in other churches of the district, as at Landewednack and St. Mawgan [f].

The font is supported by a central pillar and four slender shafts; the bowl has a circular form of ornamentation similar to that on the font at St. Levan [g].

[f] It is remarkable that precisely the same arrangement is common in Pembrokeshire, and one very similar to it in Somersetshire and other parts of the country.

[g] GENT. MAG., April, 1862, p. 394.

The tower, of two stages, has battlements and pinnacles: it is constructed entirely of granite, which material must have been brought from a considerable distance. The mullions of the windows and the piers are also of granite.

There are three bells in the tower; the oldest is dated 1761, and has for its legend "Jesus de Nazareth Rex Judaeorum."

Either Cury Church, or that of Menheniot, in East Cornwall (for both are named after St. Corantyne), was the first in which the Liturgy was read in English. Dr. Whitaker says it was Menheniot.

Exterior of Low Side Window, Cury.

St. Cury Church is now in a state of good repair, the late incumbent, the Rev. Saltren Rogers, now Vicar of Gwennap, having done much to restore it to its original appearance.

In the south part of the churchyard is an ancient cross of granite, nine feet high, one of the tallest monolith crosses in Cornwall [h].

[h] See Blight's "Crosses, &c., in West Cornwall," p. 36.

A mile westward from Cury is the strangely-situated church of GUNWALLOE; the coast here is formed by sand hills, called *towans*, overgrown with herbage.

Gunwalloe Church.

Those who have visited Gunwalloe Cove will agree with the Rev. C. A. Johns, who says, in his "Week at the Lizard," that it is "as delightful a spot in which to spend a long summer's day as can be well imagined." Though so lovely in summer, the winter storms that have blown on the coast have caused many a shipwreck here. In 1862 could be seen on the smooth beach of sand of the little adjoining cove of Poljew, portions of a ship which was driven on the coast but two or three months before: after striking on the rocks she broke in two. The crew remained on the fore part, and effected a landing on a huge isolated rock; thirteen, however, were washed off before aid could be rendered. It is a singular fact,—and shews by what a narrow chance lives may be lost or saved in such moments of extreme danger, when men "are at their wit's end,"—that the whole crew might have been saved had they retreated to the after part of the ship; for when the storm abated articles perfectly dry were taken out of the cabin. This is but one instance of the many wrecks that have occurred near the spot. No apology is needed for alluding to these tales of misery, for the church itself is said to have been erected as a votive offering by one who here escaped from shipwreck. Where he had been miraculously rescued from the fury of the mighty deep, he vowed that he would build a chapel in which the sounds of prayer and praise to God should blend with the never-ceasing voice of those waves from which he had so narrowly escaped. So near to the sea is the church, that at times it is reached by the spray, and the waves have frequently broken away the walls of the churchyard.

There is no reason to doubt the truth of the above tradition. Another which attempts to account for the situation of the church will not, perhaps, be so readily credited. It is said that the builders intended to erect the church on higher ground, nearer the centre of the parish, at Hingey; but as fast as materials were brought to the place they were, by some mysterious agency, removed during the night to the present site. And here the church was built, it being found useless to contend with a supernatural power.

Dr. Whitaker tells us that St. Winwaloc, or Wynwallow, the patron of the church, was a Cornishman, and that he resided on this part of the coast as a hermit. Others state that he was of noble Welsh extraction, and became Abbot of Landevenech in Bretagne, where he died in 529.

In the Taxation of Pope Nicholas IV. (A.D. 1288—1291), this church is referred to as "Ecclesia Sancti Wynwolay;" "that is," says Hals, absurdly, "the church of the holy, victorious, or conquering Wallo." In Wolsey's Inquisition, 1521, it is given in valuation and consolidation with Breage, Germoe, and Cury, by the name of the vicarage of Wynnanton. The manor of Wynnanton, or Winington, formerly claimed jurisdiction by sea and land over the whole parish.

Not only is the church most unusual in its situation, but it has the peculiar arrangement of a detached belfry, built on the solid rock against a steep ascent westward of the church. The rock forms a large portion of the west, north, and south walls. There is no tradition relating to the belfry; probably, however, funds were not available for the building of a tower to the church, and this was erected as a temporary receptacle for the bells.

Two of the bells appear to be of early date. One has this legend:—

"Voce mea viva depello cuncta nociva."—"With my living voice I drive away all hurtful things[1]."

[1] The same inscription appears on a bell of the fourteenth century at the parish church of All Hallows, Ringmore, South Devon.

On the middle bell:—

"Ichs ois plaudit ut me tam sepius audit."—Which may be read, "Jesus is praised by all as often as my voice is heard."

The third and latest bears the following:—

"Eternis annis resonet campana Johannis."—"Let the bell of [St.] John resound in endless years."

The church is of the fifteenth century, and consists of a chancel, nave, north and south aisles, and a south porch. Internally it is coated with whitewash, and sadly requires restoration. Its dimensions are 54 ft. by 43 ft. The belfry is fourteen feet from the church, its north-east angle being in a line with the south-west angle of the south aisle.

The open oak roof of the south aisle is particularly good, and the ribs of the porch-roof appear to have been elaborately carved. The piers, resembling those at Cury, have capitals of different design; some consist simply of a sort of twisted or cable moulding.

The side windows of the north aisle are each of two ogee-headed lights, the head filled with a quatrefoil.

The south aisle is lighted by six windows, five of which contain three round-headed lights; the west window has but two.

Behind the south and north doors are panels with carved framework, containing very rude paintings of the Apostles, with their emblems,—St. John holding a chalice with a serpent issuing from it, St. James the Great with his staff and scrip, St. Matthew holding an axe, &c. This work originally formed the lower part of the rood-screen.

The font is of late character, but in the churchyard is the fragment of an older one of much superior design, and apparently of Norman date.

Fragment of Font, Gunwalloe.

A tombstone in the churchyard has the following:—

> "We shall die all,
> Shall die all wee;
> Die all we shall,
> All we shall die."

MULLION CHURCH is about half an hour's walk from Gunwalloe. Its plan is the same as that of Gunwalloe, except that the tower is joined to the west end of the nave. This tower is said to have been erected in the year 1500 at the expense of Mr. Robert Luddra [k]; who also at that time restored the chancel, as a curious inscription on the cornice testifies. The tower, like others in this district, is built partly of granite and partly of a sort of inferior serpentine: the light colour of the former, contrasted with the blackness of the latter, gives to the building a strange and variegated appearance. Mr. Davies

---

[k] "Robertus Ludder" is entered as Vicar in the *Valor Ecclesiasticus*—Return of Vesey, Bishop of Exeter, June 3, 1536.

Gilbert must certainly have had some authority for stating, as he has done, that the tower was erected in 1500. If, however, it were erected at that time, fragments of older work must have been used in its construction.

Over the west window, and immediately under the string-course, is a piece of granite on which is carved the Crucifixion, treated in a manner common enough in some parts of the kingdom, but of unusual occurrence in the churches of this part of Cornwall, though found on some of the later Cornish crosses.

Crucifix, Mullion Tower.

The Father, over whose head is the encircling arc of heaven, holds forth the crucified Son, who has a figure on His right hand and on His left: these, probably, are intended for the Blessed Virgin and St. John.

The hoodmould over the arched doorway springs from two corbel-heads, one of which represents the mitred head of a bishop. The tower is about 40 ft. high, and contains three

Corbel-head, Mullion Tower.

bells of modern date, said to have been cast with the metal of older ones. Tradition says that one of the ancient bells was of an unusually large size, and that it was intended for St. Kevern Church, but by some mishap in its carriage, or through the intervention of the patron saint, it fell to the lot of Mullion tower.

The windows of this church originally contained painted glass, representing among other devices the arms of De Ferrers, and of the Erisey family. The fragments that remained were collected together and inserted in the new east window, when the Rev. Francis Gregory, the late lamented vicar, restored the chancel in 1840.

The side windows of the aisles have arched heads, very depressed; the east windows have a kind of rude geometrical tracery.

Stoup, Mullion.

Bench-end, Mullion.

The door-jambs of the porch are panelled, resembling those at Gunwalloe; and the stoup remains in good preservation.

This church is particularly worthy of notice, because it retains a large proportion of the original benches, carved in a manner much superior to those in any other church in the western part of Cornwall. The designs are varied, and some are remarkable, representing soldiers, monks, heads of Bacchanalian figures, and initial letters quaintly conceived.

In the western part of the nave the arms of the Passion are beautifully represented, following in the order shewn by the accompanying cut. Beginning with the sacred characters I H C, each shield in the

Arms of the Passion, Mullion.

most suggestive manner tells some fact connected with the crucifixion of our Lord. There is the scourge; the symbol of the five wounds; the cross encircled by the crown of thorns; the initial letter of the word "Christ;" the spear of Longinus placed diagonally with the reed, on which is the sponge—arranged triangularly with these are three dice;

the ladder, with the torches; the weapons mentioned in St. John's Gospel, (chap. xviii. 3); the four nails, hammer, and pincers; the series most appropriately concluding with a shield bearing the chalice and sacramental wafer.

Shields on other benches bear the fleur-de-lis, St. Andrew's cross, and a Latin cross with the spear on one side and the reed on the other. The cross, in most instances, in this, as well as in other churches, stands on a Calvary of steps, three in number. The Rev. R. S. Hawker says,—"The three steps which lead up to a cross are symbolic of those three Christian graces of Faith, Hope, and Charity, which a penitent should seek and find whenever he pleads for pardon there."

The font is octagonal, with panelled sides. On one side the lower part of the bowl is not bevelled, like the others, but the stone extends downwards to the shaft, as if the font had been left in an unfinished state, or had been built against a wall or pillar.

On the front of the altar are two figures carved in wood, each having one hand raised to bless. One of these

Carving on the Altar, Mullion.

—evidently intended for St. Clare[1]—stands at the entrance of an ecclesiastical structure, and holds a monstrance in her right hand. These carvings formed part of the roodscreen.

Until recently the church was disfigured by an unsightly gallery at the west end of the nave, erected for the choir; this has been taken down, and other improvements made: still the building is by no means completely restored; two or three ungainly pews should be removed. Indeed, at a comparatively trifling cost it might be made one of the neatest churches in the district.

In the chancel is a tablet to the memory of Thomas Flavel, at one time vicar of the parish. Beneath the tablet on a piece of brass are the following lines :—

> " Earth take thine Earth, my Sin let Satan havet ;
> The World my Goods ; my Soul, my God, who gavet.
> For from these four—Earth, Satan, World, and God—
> My flesh, my Sin, my goods, my Soul I had."

This church is dedicated to St. Melanus, an abbot of Bretagne, born in South Wales, and the bosom friend of St. Sampson; he died about 617. St. Mellion Church, near Southill, in East Cornwall, is also dedicated to him, Southill Church being dedicated to St. Sampson.

---

[1] In this parish is an estate called Clahar (pronounced Clare) Garden, on which are the remains of an ancient chapel, similar to others in Cornwall. This was probably a chapel of St. Clare, and gave name to the estate, whence St. Clare is represented in the parish church.

In the Taxation of Pope Nicholas IV. Mullion Church is entered as "Ecclesia Sancti Melany," but in the *Valor Ecclesiasticus (temp.* Hen. VIII.), as "Vicaria de Melyan;" a connecting link this, between the original dedication, "Melan," and the curious modern corruption, "Mullion."

IV. ST. KEVERNE—MANACCAN—ST. MAWGAN.

AMONG other interpretations of the word 'Meneage,' given at p. 44, was *mean-ake,* 'the deaf stone.' The reason given for this rendering is, that though there are several mineral veins or lodes in the district, on trial they have been found of little value, and are called *deaf,* or barren. What greater punishment could be inflicted on Cornish-men than depriving their native soil of the precious ore which gives employment to some and fortunes to others? This did St. Keverne. For the irreligion of the inhabitants, and their disrespect towards him, he pronounced a curse against them, and caused the mineral veins to be unproductive; and tradition has handed down the proverb, that "no metal will run within the sound of St. Keverne's bell [m]."

There appears to be no record of a saint of the name of Keverne, but Leland, Tanner, and Dr. Whitaker have treated St. Kieran, St. Pieran, and St. Keverne as the same person. Dr. Borlase, however, was of opinion that Piran, or Pieran, and Kiaran, Kieran, or Keverne, were different personages. In

---

[m] Polwhele's Hist. of Cornwall.

Domesday Book is the following entry:—"Canonici Sancti Achebranni tenent Lannachebran, et tenebant tempore regis Edwardi." Dr. Borlase says, "The letter *a* before Chebran is no more than a preposition in the Cornish language, signifying 'of,' prefixed to the St. Chebran, or Kevran." Thus Lannachebran would be 'the church of [St.] Chebran.'

Whether Pieran, Kieran, and Chebran are to be identified as one person or not, it is evident that the Lannachebran of Domesday Book refers to the present St. Keverne, as Dr. Whitaker conclusively remarks:—

"The want of a parish for the Lannachebran of Domesday Book, and the want of a notice in Domesday Book for the parish of St. Keverne, unite to shew the one is omitted because the other is mentioned, and the one is mentioned under the name of the other."

Dr. Oliver, whose authority may be regarded as almost conclusive, does not doubt that St. Keverne was collegiate; and he further informs us that—

"This property was granted by Richard, Earl of Cornwall, to his father's foundation of Beaulieu, Hants., and was confirmed to that monastery by Bishop Brewer, and by Pope Gregory IX. In 30 Edward I. that abbey was allowed by the justices in eyre extensive liberties in their vill of St. 'Keveran' under the grants of the two preceding kings. Until the dissolution of religious houses the vicars of St. Keverne were presented by the abbot and convent of that Cistercian abbey. After the transfer of the property to the abbey, the church does not appear to have retained its collegiate character. . . . . Bishop Bronescombe, June 10, 1266, admitted William Postjoye to this vicarage, reserving to the abbey of Beaulieu the whole tithe of the fishery, and the tithe of beans, peas, and vetches, and of all other things growing within the fields of the parish[n]."

[n] Oliver's *Monasticon*.

Leland says:—

"Within the land of Meneke, or Menegland, is a Paroch Chirch of St. Keueryn, otherwis Piranus; and ther is a sanctuary with x. or xii. dwelling Howses, and therby was a Sel of Monkes, but now goon home to ther Hed Hows°."

St. Keverne's is the largest church in the western part of Cornwall, being about 110 feet in length; and consists of nave, chancel, north and south aisles, tower at west end of nave, and a south porch. Dr. Whitaker considered the large dimensions of the church evidence of its "once collegiate dignity." We have seen from Dr. Oliver that the church did not retain its collegiate character after its transfer to Beaulieu Abbey. So the present church, or at least the greater portion of it, having been erected since that period, its size can have no connexion with its collegiate establishment,—unless, indeed, the church were built on the original foundations, which is not probable, for it appears to have been enlarged from time to time. The aisles are connected with the nave on either side by an arcade of eight acutely pointed arches, which give great height to the church. The piers have more elaborate mouldings than are generally found in Cornish churches, and are of four different sections; (see next page). The tower is constructed on three well-proportioned arches: those north and south open directly into the aisles, of which they may be said to form the westernmost

° C. S. Gilbert says there were six chapels in this parish.—*Hist. of Cornwall.*

bays. Surmounting the tower is a newly-built spire of the same design and proportions as the original one, which was struck down by lightning in the year 1770. The western wall of the tower is exceedingly massive, has a doorway with good mouldings, and square hoodmould with curious terminations: on each side of this mould is a shield, one of which bears three flagons or chalices.

Westward of doorway in north aisle is a small lancet-window of one light, and two probably contemporaneous buttresses, which would give an earlier date to this portion of the church. Buttresses of different character are carried along the wall; immediately adjoining the second eastward of the door is a wide projec-

Capital and Base of Pier, St. Keverne.

tion, resembling a rood-turret, and containing a blocked light, 1 ft. by 6 in., and 3 ft. 6 in. from the ground; (A in plan). Internally, the wall being plastered, there is no evidence to shew whether this contains a staircase; if it does not, the small light is a remarkable feature, and may have been a confessional window. It is probable, however, that the turret was for the staircase of the roodloft, which, if the church was subsequently extended eastward, was also moved in that direction, for there is still an

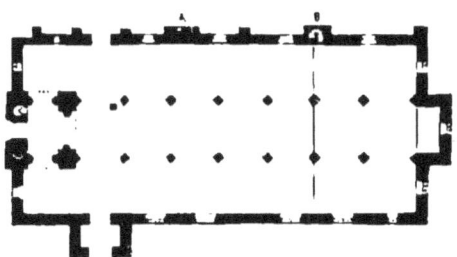

Plan of St. Keverne Church.

undoubted rood-turret nearer the eastern end of this wall; (B in plan).

With the exception of the lancet, all the windows are large, of three, four, and five lights, and of Perpendicular character.

Several of the original benches remain in the western part of the nave and north aisle; they have an appearance of great age, and may be coeval with the portions of the church in which they are situated. The carvings represent, chiefly, the arms of the Passion; some of the most remarkable of which are shewn in the opposite cut.

On every standard are two shields, each, in most instances, having reference to the same personage or object. Of those here figured, the first represents two nails—it is very unusual to find only two nails given. The others appear to be the pillar; the cord (on one shield these are given together, the cord forming a circle over the pillar); the ladder;

the spear and scourge; the sacred heart pierced by
the spear; a monogram of the B.V.M.; crowned

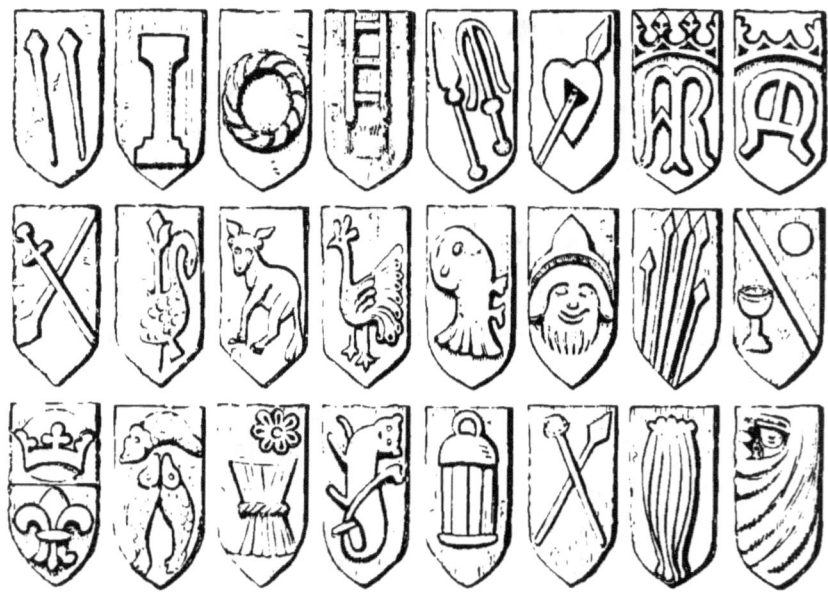

Shields on Bench-ends, St. Keverne.

initial letter of the word "Mary;" the sword and
spear. The next two shields appear to have reference to the blessed Virgin, from the curiously formed
fleur-de-lis, a portion of which is broken away. The
two following have reference to St. Peter,—the cock
which called him to repentance, and the fish from
which he took the tribute-money. The next figure
is probably intended for Pontius Pilate, his authority
or governorship being expressed by the number of
spears on the following shield. The next two are

the chalice and sacramental wafer, the fleur-de-lis and crown of the blessed Virgin. The meaning of some of the others is not very evident; on the fifth and sixth shields in this line are the lantern, spear, and reed with sponge; the last two possibly refer to the body of our Lord, being "wrapped in linen."

There is a tradition that the oak out of which these benches are carved grew on Crowza-downs, now a dreary tract and wilderness of rocks. Those who know the spot will scarcely believe the truth of the tradition.

The font has an octagonal bowl, with four angels at the angles; the breast of each being crossed by bands forming a St. Andrew's cross. On four of the sides are the initials A.M., and the sacred monogram I.H.S. The bowl is supported on a square shaft, curved inwardly; this feature appears peculiar to some of the fonts of the district [p].

[p] In the north aisle is an elaborate monument to the memory of "Maj.-Gen. H. C. Cavendish, Capt. S. G. Dunkenfield, Lieut. the Hon. Edward Waldegrave, and 61 non-commissioned officers and privates of the . . . Regiment, who, in returning from Spain in the 'Dispatch' transport, unhappily perished in Coverack Cove, the 22nd of Jan., 1809."

In the south aisle are the arms of Incledon, the famous singer, a native of this parish. In the same aisle is an epitaph to Thomas Toll, concluding with an anagram—

"Anag. { Thomas / Toll } Smooth Tall.

"In converse smooth, faire, plaine, and voide of guile,
Of Stature Tall; whose loss we do bewaile."

The date of this is 1668, and it may be considered a good example of the prevailing taste of the period.

Cornish Churches. 67

MANACCAN CHURCH, about four miles from St. Keverne, is beautifully situated on wooded land rising above the Durra, a creek parallel with the

Plan of Manaccan Church. Scale, 25 ft. to 1 in.

Helford river. It has several features of interest, and goes far to prove that most of the Cornish churches which now consist of nave, chancel, one aisle, and one transept,—the aisle having superseded a transept,— were originally cruciform.

The chancel and transept are of the same date—Early English. The east window of the chancel is a triple lancet, the two south windows are single lancets. There is a single lancet, of precisely the same character as the chancel windows, in the east wall of the transept, and the window in the

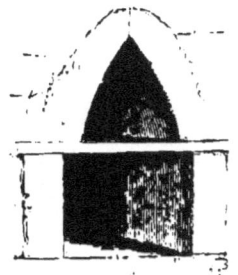

Piscina in Transept, Manaccan.

south wall of the transept was originally a double lancet. The piscina near the east window of the transept also proves its Early English character.

The present roof of the chancel appears to be the original one; it is shewn in the accompanying view of the interior. The principals on the north side are

Interior of Chancel, Manaccan.

good evidence of the existence of a north transept, otherwise there could have been no necessity for such a construction. On the north side of the chancel are six corbels, sculptured with crosses, quatrefoils, and other devices; these support that portion of the wall-plate which was disturbed when the north aisle was added. The nave is wider than the chancel, and the arches being necessarily in a line with the nave, these corbels were required for the then overhanging-roof;

but whether they were sculptured at that time, or older work used up, is uncertain; not more than two have any similarity of design or shape.

The angle formed by the east wall of the transept and the south wall of the chancel terminates in a piece of granite, broadly chamfered, which supported the roodloft; to the east of this a doorway is plainly discernible beneath the plastering, which, taken in connexion with the evident disturbance of the walls of the angle externally, shews there was a hagioscopic passage here similar to others in the district. From

South-east View of Chancel and Transept, Manaccan.

this angle, as far as the sacrarium step, there appears to have been something like a stone bench constructed against or built with the wall; it was eighteen inches high. It has been suggested whether this was a bench carried around the walls of the church, as at Tintagel, of which the chancel only remains. But

South Doorway, Manaccan.

there can be little doubt as to the transept being

contemporaneous with the chancel. Then west of the transept is still earlier work. The south doorway is one of the best Norman doorways in Cornwall, and is perhaps an early example of that style of architecture [q]. (See opposite page.)

The tower is of two stages, battlemented and pinnacled: the entrance to the staircase is unusually placed, being direct from the nave, and the first step 7 ft. 6 in. from the floor.

The bowl of the old font is preserved in the vicarage grounds.

A peculiar feature in connexion with this church is a large fig-tree—diameter of trunk about 10 in.—growing out of the south wall of the nave. A fig-tree also grows in the western wall of Newlyn Church, in East Cornwall.

Dr. Oliver calls Manaccan *Manacon* or *Monathon*, and says the church is dedicated to St. Antoninus.

[q] The Rev. Edward Budge, at one time Vicar of Manaccan, published an account of this doorway in the Reports of the Royal Institution of Cornwall (1846), and states with much plausibility that the crimp moulding carried round the two arches is the original type of the zigzag so characteristic of Norman architecture; "and that it was suggested by the obvious device of placing a succession of bricks on their sides in a row, each one alternately projecting a little beyond the other, which we still see done occasionally in modern masonry to form a sort of rude cornice, as round the tops of chimneys for instance. Supposing a row of bricks placed in the manner just described, the corners of each will stand out in angular projection very much like the crimp seen in the cubes of this doorway. The profile of this figure is evidently the zigzag."

The present Vicar, the Rev. Edward Seymour[r], has with much good taste improved the chancel of this church, which was, in common with others of this neighbourhood, in a deplorable state.

ST. MAWGAN IN KERRIER is of the same plan as Manaccan, and was originally cruciform, the north transept having been removed for the north aisle.

The east chancel-window and the south window of the transept are each of good flowing Decorated, of three lights. All the other windows are late.

The roofs of the chancel and the nave are of the usual cradle form, and plastered; the roof of the aisle richly carved woodwork.

At the angle of the transept and chancel is a hagioscope of similar plan to that at Cury and other

Hagioscope, St. Mawgan.

---

[r] I would take this opportunity of acknowledging the valuable aid Mr. Seymour has given me in preparing these notes and sketches of Manaccan Church.

churches in the district; it is, however, superior to the others, and differs in detail: the slender octagonal shaft supporting the north arch is peculiar. There is a plain shield over the eastern side of the capital of this shaft, and on the capital of the large detached octagonal shaft is a figure holding a shield. The dimensions of the low side window are 2 ft. 2 in. by 1 ft. 1 in.; it is 4 ft. 6 in. from the floor. A vestry unfortunately having been built to the east side of the transept, the window is blocked, and the external arrangement of the angle destroyed.

The south wall of the transept has two low buttresses,—an unusual feature; internally, beneath the window is a large mural arch, having shafts with capitals. It appears to have been constructed for the reception of an effigy, though not now occupied. Near it, however, are two effigies of stone, each about 6 ft. long, representing a Crusader and his lady (see p. 74). These, according to some of the county historians, were removed hither, when the church was built, from a little chapel in this parish belonging to the Carminow family. Hals says they were removed in the reign of King James I., and refers to inscriptions. But C. S. Gilbert, who alludes to these effigies as laid "in the recess," thought it "more probable that they were brought from the church of the Grey Friars at Bodmin, where figures of the kind are known to have laid in commemoration of the Carminow family." And in his account of that family he particularly mentions one Oliver Carminow as a person of great note in the time of Richard II., to whom he had the honour of being Lord Chamberlain. "He

Effigies, St. Mawgan.

died, apparently very aged, in 1395, and was buried, together with Elizabeth his lady, sister of John Holland, Duke of Exeter, in the church of the Grey Friars at Bodmin, where they were for some time represented in effigy, she with a coronet and he with his legs across." According to Hals there was a tradition which said that one Robert de Carmynow "accompanied King Edward I. in the holy war in Palestine." Undoubtedly this was one of the most ancient of Cornish families; indeed, there is a tradition that one of the Carminows fought at the landing of Julius Cæsar, and it will be remembered that during the celebrated Scrope and Grosvenor controversy the disputed arms were claimed by the Carminows as theirs from Saxon days! The Crusader in St. Mawgan Church, and represented by the engraving on p. 74, is certainly a Carminow, for he bears their arms, "Azure, a bend or," and may be the effigy of that "Robert de Carmynow" mentioned by Hals. The transept is called "the Carminow aisle."

The tower, of three stages, is the finest in this part of the county; the pinnacles are formed by clustered shafts, are crocketed and finialed, and rest on corbels carved as angels of evil. The belfry windows are of three lights, as is also the western window. On the keystone of the arch of the latter is carved a figure resembling a bishop holding a staff or crozier; on each stone at the springings of the arch is carved a shield, one of which is represented by the annexed cut. On the three principal stones of the doorway-arch shields are also sculptured; one has the figure of a

Keystone, Tower Window, St. Mawgan.

Shields on Tower, St. Mawgan.

crescent, another a lion with two horse-shoes, as shewn on p. 75. Hals says that on the tower of St. Mawgan are sculptured the arms of the families of Carminow, Reskymer, Ferrers, and Vyvyan. The jambs of the doorway are carved with a continuous pattern of foliage, which springs from the head of a king and queen. The tower-arch is admirably proportioned, and springs from two curious corbels—figures holding shields. The keystone is peculiar, terminating in a round flat disc, on which is sculptured, very sharply though not in great relief, a plain Latin cross, a figure resembling the spear and sponge, a pair of compasses, and a circular disc.

Jamb of Tower-door, St. Mawgan.

The font is octagonal, with a shaft curved inwardly, and four circular slender shafts attached, following the curve.

The aisle appears to be of the fifteenth century, and opens into the nave and chancel by an arcade of seven four-centred arches. The piers are of the usual style, shafted at the angles, and with hollow mouldings. The capitals are rudely carved and vary in design, some having foliage, others cables intertwined.

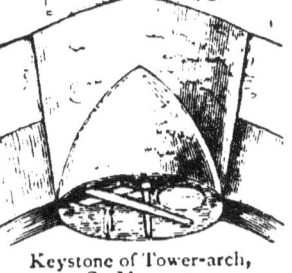

Keystone of Tower-arch, St. Mawgan.

On the north side of the aisle is a small transeptal projection used as a pew by the Vyvyan family, of which it contains monuments, one a marble slab to the memory of Sir Vyell Vyvyan, Bart. In the eastern part of the aisle are a helmet and sword said to have been worn by Sir Richard Vyvyan, fighting loyally, in the Great Rebellion.

This church is dedicated to St. Mauganus.

V. ST. ANTONY, LANDEWEDNACK—ST. RUAN MAJOR.

THE parish of ST. ANTONY IN KIRRIER occupies a mere neck of land, bounded on one side by the Helford River, and on the other by the Durra. The church, embosomed in trees, and almost close to the water's edge, stands on the southern side of the narrowest part of the promontory, the extreme eastern point of which is cut off by an ancient earthwork, Castle Dinas, which was occupied during the Great Rebellion, and surrendered to Sir Thomas Fairfax in 1646. It was the last place in Cornwall held for the King, except St. Michael's Mount and Pendennis Castle, and was defended by Sir Richard Vyvyan.

The situation of the church is very peculiar, and has a legend attached similar to that of Gunwalloe. It is said that soon after the Conquest, as some Normans of rank were crossing from Normandy into England, a tempest drove them on the Cornish coast, where they were in momentary danger of destruction; but in their distress they called on St. Antony, and vowed if he would save them from shipwreck they would build a church in his honour on the spot where they should first land. The ship was wafted into the Durra creek, and there the pious Normans as soon as possible fulfilled their vow. As in those days men were more wont than at the present time to express their gratitude to God in some visible form, this story seems not improbable, and a votive chapel may have marked the site for the present Church.

This parish is not mentioned in Domesday Book, but Bishop Tanner says there was a cell of Black Monks of Angiers here, belonging to the Priory of Tywardreath, which existed as early as the reign of Richard I. Its site is supposed to have been on an estate called Lantinny, adjoining the churchyard, where foundations of buildings and remains of human bodies have been found[s]. Dugdale also refers to St. Antony (or Antonine) in Meneage as a cell to Tywardreath, and says that "being mentioned in Gervase of Canterbury's Catalogue, it must have existed as early as the time of King Richard I." It is rated in the Pope's Inquisition of 1294. Dr. Oliver says the church is dedicated to Antoninus the Martyr, but gives no date of dedication.

The plan of the existing church closely resembles that of Manaccan: consisting of a chancel, nave,

[s] Lysons' "Cornwall."

north aisle, tower at the west end of the nave, and a shallow south transept with porch adjoining it to

The Church of St. Antony in Kirrier.

the west. The chancel appears to be of much earlier date than any other portions of the building, and has on its north side a single lancet, partially blocked. The east windows of the chancel and aisle are both good Early Perpendicular (see next page). With the exception of a small single-light on the south side of the chancel, and a window of three lights trefoliated in the transept, all the others are of two lights, under a square hood-mould.

The nave and aisle are divided by an arcade of five acutely pointed arches, one side of each arch being formed by a single piece of granite, with mouldings of a simple order. The piers are plain octagonal shafts, with capitals of the same form.

Window of Chancel and East Window of Aisle, St. Antony.

The rood-turret on the north side of the aisle is very remarkable in having the entrance to the stairs on the outside. The north wall of the aisle is buttressed, and there are two buttresses against the south wall of the chancel.

The tower, of three stages, battlemented and pinnacled, and between sixty and seventy feet high, somewhat resembles that of St. Mawgan, though not so elaborately ornamented: it is built of granite.

The pinnacles are formed by clustered shafts resting on angels. The belfry windows, of unusually large size for the district, are of three lights, with geometrical tracery. The western doorway consists of a depressed four-centred arch within a square head, the spandrels being filled with a trefoil ornament. The tower-arch, simply a plain soffit, is semicircular.

The font, standing in the western end of the aisle, appears to be of the thirteenth century, and, like many others in Cornwall, has around the bowl four angels bearing shields. Around the upper part of the bowl is an inscription—" Ecce karissimi de Deo vero baptizabuntur spiritu sancto," with the initials Q. P., B. M., B. V., P. R.; two letters being placed between each angel. Height of the font, including base, 3 ft. 3 in.[t]

Font, St. Antony.

The Perpendicular additions to this church are mostly of early and good character.

[t] In Lysons' "Cornwall" will be found an engraving of a font, formerly in Camborne Church, similar to this, and with the same inscription.

LANDEWEDNACK, the most southerly church in England, is little more than a mile north-east from the Lizard Point, and stands near the summit of a slope terminating at the cliffs about a furlong distant. Nothing can be more beautiful than the situation of this church and its churchyard. The murmuring of the sea below can be distinctly heard; and between the trunks of the trees, by which the church is surrounded, are glimpses of its deep blue, dotted here and there with the white sails of the outward or homeward bound. But tombstones in this grassy slope tell of many a bark which, on the rugged coast, untimely finished its course, and of those who perished on the dark crags. In fact, we have here the usual tales told on stone in most seaside churchyards.

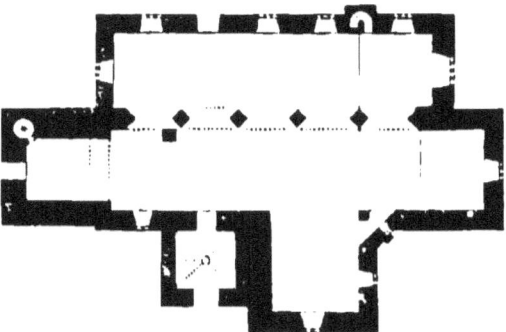

Plan of Landewednack Church.

The plan of this church also very nearly resembles Manaccan; but here, as at St. Antony, the porch adjoins the transept, and this latter has the peculiar hagioscopic arrangement in the angle, similar to those already noticed at St. Cury and St. Mawgan. The low side window, however, is of two lights; and just beneath it, from the foundation of the wall, into which it is built, projects a rude block of stone, which might have been convenient for persons to stand on if these windows really had an outward use. At St. Cury are no traces of the existence of such a block.

Exterior of Low Side Window, Landewednack.

The dimensions of the window are 2 ft. 10 in. by 1 ft. 8 in.; the sill 5 ft. from the ground; from the sill to the stone beneath it, 4 ft. $3\frac{1}{2}$ in.; breadth of the wall, 4 ft. The internal arrangement is nearly the same as at St. Cury[u].

[u] In the GENTLEMAN'S MAGAZINE, vol. cci. pp. 543, 544, will be found a plan of Bosherston Church, Pembroke, with view of a squint similar to that at Landewednack. At the former, however, the oblique wall appears to be of greater length, and the small window occupies a more central position. The lean-to roof is in each case arranged in just the same manner. Landewednack was most probably originally a cruciform church, like that at Bosherston.

The chancel and transept appear to be contemporaneous: in each are piscina niches of the same form—simply an arched recess; the basins are gone. The windows of the chancel, transept, and nave are of Decorated character, as is also the porch—a most remarkable structure to find attached to a church in Cornwall, where groining and stone ribs are very rare. The vault runs north and south, and has boldly chamfered diagonal and cross ribs; the former supported by angels bearing shields, and the whole terminating in a central boss—an angel holding a scroll. The outer entrance has a segmental arch, and the walls are battlemented. The inner doorway

Boss on Porch, Landewednack.

has considerable remains of Norman work; indeed, the Norman doorway is complete of itself, but a Perpendicular doorway has been constructed within it, and from the segmental arch and niche for image there appears to have been a doorway occupying the space previous to the present one, possibly contemporaneous with the porch itself. The Norman doorway is of most unusually lofty proportions, being 9 ft. high, and 4 ft. 5 in. from jamb to jamb: the jambs are partially built of that curious sandstone which has been referred to as existing in early work at St. Levan and St. Burian; it almost resembles a concrete, and may, with the back of a

South Doorway, Landewednack.

penknife, be scraped into particles of sand as it originally existed. The positions of these stones—two on the left, and one forming part of the base of the right shaft—are indicated in the engraving, p. 85. The same material is used in the formation of the piscina in the chancel.

The font supported on a central pillar and four shafts, a form frequently met with in Cornwall, is probably of the thirteenth century, and bears an inscription in early English characters, "I. H. C. D. Ric. (Dominus Ricardus) Bolham me fecit."

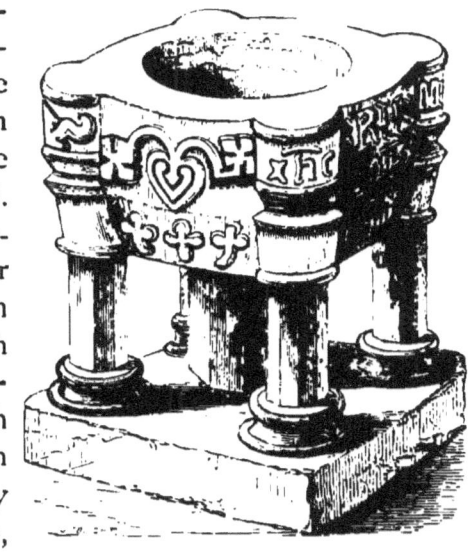

Font, Landewednack.

The tower, built perhaps early in the fifteenth century, is of two stages, unbuttressed; it is battlemented

Inscription on the Font, Landewednack.

and has crocketed pinnacles. The doorway is blocked. The western window of three lights, and the belfry lights under square hoodmoulds, are constructed of granite. The same material is used in other parts of the tower, and in conjunction with the dark stone of the district has a singular effect. The staircase, as usual, is contained in the thickness of the north wall. The tower-arch has a plain soffit. There are three bells, apparently of early date; they bear the following legends:—

> "Sancta Anna ora pro nobis."
> "Sancte Nicholas ora pro nobis."
> "Nomen Magdalene gerit campana melodie."

The founder's mark—a bell, with the initials B. V.—is the same on the north and south bells, and is met with in other parts of the kingdom. The shields on the bell of St. Nicholas do not, however, seem to be familiar to the collectors of bell-marks.

On North and South Bells,
Landewednack.

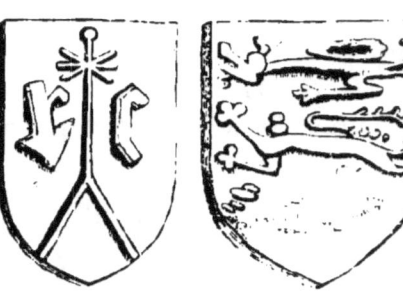

On the Bell St. Nicholas,
Landewednack.

An exceedingly fine sea-view may be had from the roof of the tower.

The aisle, added late in the fifteenth or in the beginning of the sixteenth century, has no features of interest.

The present Rector, the Rev. Philip Vyvyan Robinson, has put the chancel in order, erected a polished serpentine pulpit, opened the tower-arch, and effected other improvements. The rich colours of the serpentine stone render it very effective for interior fittings of churches, and it is now being much used for that purpose.

In the churchyard—perhaps the only instance of the kind—are tombstones of polished serpentine.

According to Dr. Borlase, the last sermon in the Cornish language was preached in Landewednack Church, not long before the year 1678, by the rector, the Rev. F. Robinson. After the language ceased to be used in churches it soon became extinct. "Had the Liturgy," says Dr. Whitaker, "been translated into Cornish, as it was into Welsh, that language would have been equally preserved with this to the present moment." And the Doctor remarks, with much indignation, that an English Liturgy "was not desired by the Cornish, but forced upon them by the tyranny of England, at a time when the English language was yet unknown in Cornwall."

Dr. Oliver says the church is dedicated to St. Winwolus—the same as Gunwalloe. It is difficult to imagine how Winwolus, or Winwoluc, could be corrupted into Wednack, as some have conjectured. The present name evidently had the same origin as Landevenach in Bretagne.

On the flat open country, little more than two miles from Landewednack, stands the Church of ST. RUAN MAJOR, surrounded by trees, which shelter it from the winds to which the neighbouring lands are terribly exposed. Somewhere on this tract is supposed to have existed the Nemean wood, in which St. Rumon, the patron of the church, had his cell, and passed the greater number of his days[x]. It appears that he came over from Ireland, and sought this retired spot for the solitude and contemplation of a hermit's life. Near the church of St. Grade is a village named St. Ruan, where there was a small ecclesiastical structure. This is pointed at as the exact spot of the Saint's residence. His well was two or three hundred yards distant, and may still be seen, having been in mediæval times enclosed by walls, with a ribbed roof and pointed archway. From this retreat Dr. Whitaker contends that St. Rumon was taken to become one of the early bishops of Cornwall, but that he soon returned to his hermitage, where he died, "was buried in his oratory, and then became sainted by the reverence of the country adjoining." Ordulph, Duke of Cornwall, knowing how Rumon was reverenced, caused the Saint's bones to be removed to the monastery which he founded at Tavistock, A.D. 961[y]. And so greatly was the Saint

---

[x] "Rumonus genere fuit Scotus Hiberniensis. Nemea sylva in Cornubia, plenissima olim ferarum. S. Rumonus faciebat sibi oratorium in sylva Nemæa. Falemutha."—*Leland's Collect.*, tom. iv. p. 153.

[y] "King William II., A.D. 1096, in the ninth year of his reign, con-

esteemed in the vicinity of his abode, that two churches were there consecrated to his name, and are now distinguished by the titles of St. Ruan Major and St. Ruan Minor.

St. Ruan Major consists of a chancel, nave, north and south aisles, a south porch, and western tower. The chancel, projecting one bay beyond the aisles, is the oldest part of the church, and, as at St. Antony, has a single lancet on the north and south sides. The east window, a late insertion, consists of three ogee lights under a very depressed head. The two easternmost windows in the side of the south aisle are Decorated, of two lights, the head of one being filled with a trefoil. Some of the other windows of the aisle are of good Perpendicular. Over that in the western gable is a corbel-head.

Window in South Aisle, St. Ruan Major.

The gable of the porch is surmounted by a granite cross, boldly chamfered. The jambs of the outer entrance are octagonal and panelled.

firmed to this monastery the manor of Wulurinton, in Devonshire, giving seisin of it to the abbat 'per cultellum eburneum' (by the delivery of an ivory knife), in the presence of the Bishops of Winchester and Bath and Wells, and the Abbat of Glastonbury. The knife, it is added, was deposited in the shrine of St. Rumon."—*Dugdale's Monasticon*, ii. 489.

Cornish Churches. 91

In the eastern wall of the north aisle, which is probably the latest part of the church, are traces of an altar, with remains of brackets north and south. The rood-turret is of most unusual breadth—eight feet. Of the roodscreen itself some panels remain across the chancel and the north aisle. The carving is not very bold, but better finished than usual; several of the designs are on medallions. The heads of a male and female are particularly good. On one medallion the carver has represented his own tools—a pair of compasses, a mallet, and two curiously-formed instruments, apparently graving tools, one of which seems well adapted for cutting a sort of triangular notching, frequently found as a border ornament in fifteenth-century work.

On Roodscreen, St. Ruan Major.

Triangular Notching.

The most peculiar features in the church are two narrow openings formed at the junction of the nave and chancel side arcades, and immediately adjoining the screen piers (see p. 93). On the north side the easternmost pier rests on a solid block of masonry, 3 ft. 5 in. high (A); the height of the opening is 2 ft. 11 in., breadth 1 ft. 10 in. The height of the southern opening (B), which extends from the lintel to the floor, is 6 ft. 2 in., its breadth only 1 ft. 6 in., so that it could scarcely have been used as a passage from the chancel to the south chancel-aisle; whilst on the north side the passage theory would be still more improbable, owing to the low dimensions of the opening, and its height from the floor, there being no connecting steps[1]. The eastern piers are octagonal, whilst the western ones are the same as those in the nave, three-quarter rounds and cavettos.

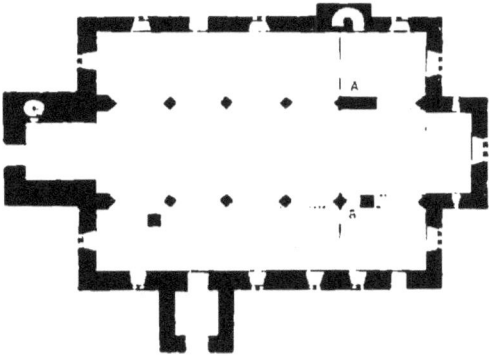

Plan of St. Ruan Major Church.

This peculiar arrangement of the aisle-churches occurs in two or three other instances in Western Cornwall. At St. Mullion the openings are nearly four feet wide, and both extend to the floor, the piers and arches being of the same character, and nearly as high as those of the nave and chancel. In no other instance are the spaces so narrow as at St. Ruan[a]. Within the screen are two carved desk-

[1] These openings were probably connected with the chantry altars at the ends of the aisles.

[a] At St. Grade Church, recently taken down, the opening on the north side was about the same breadth, 1 ft. 10 in.

ends, the slope above the square top of the standard being formed by a kneeling angel. On one panel

Openings at Junction of Chancel and Nave, St. Ruan Major.
(The dotted lines mark the position of the Roodscreen.)

is a shield with the letter R. These desks face eastward, and are in a line with the peculiar openings described above [b]. They seem to occupy their original position.

An engraving of the tower is given, as it serves to illustrate the general features of three or four towers of the Lizard district. The ground-plan is oblong, its greatest length being from north to south; dimensions, 17 ft. 10 in. by 14 ft. 10 in. outside. The height is about 45 ft. The staircase in the north-west angle

[b] These desks were probably for the use of the chantry priests.

is contained within the thickness of the wall, by which arrangement the western doorway and window are thrust southward from the centre. The tower-arch has a plain soffit. There are two stages, divided by a bold set-off, carried round the tower, after the manner of a stringcourse; the parapet, with a plain cavetto mould, overhangs the upper stage, being brought out to the plane of the base of the tower. The battlements are plain, without mouldings. The pinnacles are square and crocketed, with peculiar finials—crosses placed horizontally and diagonally to the sides of the tower. There are four belfry windows, each of two lights, with a quatrefoil in the head. The western window is Perpendicular, with three lights.

This tower, like others previously noticed, presents a singular effect from the material used in its construction; it is one of the black and white towers, ashlar blocks of dark ser-

Tower, St. Ruan Major.

pentine and coarse granite, giving the walls an irregularly chequered appearance. For the window-tracery, pinnacles, battlements, and courses, a finer granite is used, which must have been brought from a considerable distance. At St. Grade, a neighbouring parish, the tower in every respect nearly resembles that at St. Ruan, and was, according to C. S. Gilbert[c], built in the year 1400. This seems a probable date for both towers[d].

On the floor of the south aisle is a coffin-lid of red porphyry, five feet long, with a cross fleury in relief on three steps.

VI. ST. RUAN MINOR—ST. GRADE—ST. WENDRON.

ST. RUAN MINOR, the smallest church in the deanery of Kirrier, appears originally to have been a chapel, consisting only of the present chancel and nave as far as the porch, which is modern. The north aisle and tower were apparently added in the sixteenth century.

The old east window, of two lights and quatrefoiled head, has been removed to the west end of the aisle. In the south wall are two single Decorated lights, each resembling those in St. Madron tower[e].

[c] History of Cornwall, vol. ii. p. 773.
[d] A useful paper on the church towers of the Lizard district, by J. J. Rogers, Esq., M.P., was published in the Transactions of the Exeter Diocesan Architectural Society, vol. iv.
[e] See above, p. 29.

The aisle is separated from the nave and chancel by an arcade of four pointed arches. The piers, very low and massive, have three-quarter rounds and hollow mouldings, rising from the floor without bases, and with capitals different from the usual Cornish type of the same period.

Previously to the recent restorations the easternmost arch was of narrower span and not so high as the others; this marked distinction between the chantry or aisle chapel arch and aisle arcades exists in a few other churches of the district.

The tower is a very plain square structure of one stage, with a projecting battlemented parapet without pinnacles, and a pyramidal roof rising above the parapet. There are four square belfry lights, and a modern pointed west window. The tower-arch is a plain soffit. There are no stairs, the access to the belfry being by a ladder.

Piscina, St. Ruan Minor.

The basin of the piscina in the chancel looks like transition Norman inserted in a niche of later date. The font (see next page), with a plain zigzag ornament, is, perhaps, contemporaneous with the piscina basin.

The Rev. F. C. Jackson, the rector, has, with a few alterations, restored the church throughout.

Font, St. Ruan Minor.

From time immemorial, the rector of St. Ruan Minor has had the right of sending a horse into a certain field in the parish of Landewednack when t is cropped with corn, and taking away as many sheaves as the horse can carry on its back.

The very interesting church of ST. GRADE stood between St. Ruan Major and Landewednack. Being considered too dilapidated for repair, it was, about two years ago, with the exception of the tower, taken down, and a nave and chancel only erected in its place. The old church was cruciform, and had the hagioscopic arrangement in the south-east angle, and the peculiar opening like that at St. Ruan Major adjoining the roodscreen.

The middle bell in the tower bears the legend—

"O Martir Cristofore pro nobis semper orare."

The initials are very prettily crowned, and the founder's mark is the same as that on the north bell at Landewednack[f].

Though a portion of the parish of ST. WENDRON extends almost into the Lizard district, the church is situated some miles beyond the limits of the serpentine rock, and stands among the granite hills.

At certain seasons of the year this tract of country presents a dreary and barren aspect, much of the land being uncultivated, with masses of rock rising above the soil. Still, even the wildness of the scene renders it interesting; and, though perhaps not very inviting to the tourist in winter, it is beautiful at the time when the furze and heath are in bloom among the grey rocks. Many of these rocks, too, will themselves attract attention from their fantastic forms and strange positions. Then, again, there are traces of the works of Celtic days,—circles, barrows, and "giants' houses,"—respecting which the honest people of the neighbourhood tell of battles fought, of giants hurling, and of the mysteries of the Druids.

[f] See above, p. 87.

The church as it now exists has chancel, nave with western tower, north transept, and south aisle with porch. A vestry has recently been built against the western side of the transept.

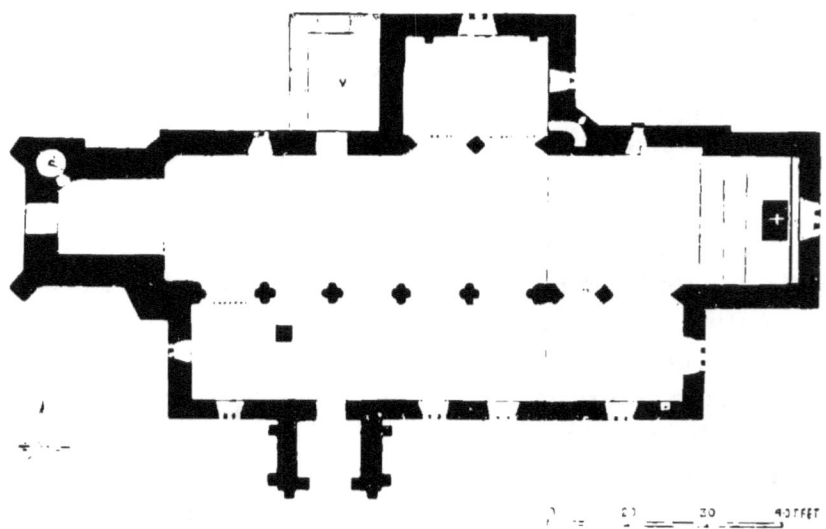

Plan of St. Wendron Church.

It would now, perhaps, be difficult to decide on what was the original plan. The chancel appears to be much older than any other portion of the building; it has some peculiar features, and is differently arranged from the chancels of other churches in the neighbourhood. It is elevated by a single step above the nave; there are three steps to the sanctuary, and behind the altar the east wall is stepped in a remarkable manner, probably indicating the site of an ancient reredos.

In the north wall, at the foot of the altar steps, is a segmental mural arch with a good moulding; it is eight feet in breadth, and forms a recess about a foot in depth (A in plan). This no doubt was an Easter sepulchre. A single-light window, eleven inches wide and six feet high, is placed over the western part of the recess. Externally, this window, as shewn in the accompanying illustration, is cut through a

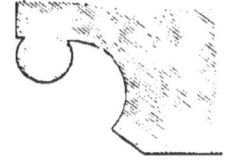

Moulding of Mural Arch, St. Wendron.

North-east View of Chancel and Transept, St. Wendron.

plinth which extends from the junction of transept and chancel to a few feet eastward of the mural arch within. This plinth was evidently constructed to increase the thickness of the wall hollowed out for the arch.

The east window is of late flowing Decorated, nearly flamboyant. In design it closely resembles the chancel window of St. Mawgan, excepting that it has no hoodmould. An unusual feature in this window is that the jambs are built with small stones, and not formed of one or two lengths, as is generally the case in west-country churches.

Between the chancel and chantry or south aisle chapel, occurs the small connecting opening, similar to those already noticed as existing in other churches of the district (B in plan). The archway is 7 ft. high and 3 ft. 8 in. wide. At the apex of the arch is a corbel, on which a portion of the roodloft rested. The arch east of the opening is of greater breadth, but not so high, as the pier-arches between nave and aisle.

East Window of Chancel, St. Wendron.

The rood staircase is contained in the angle at the junction of chancel and transept.

Though the pretty little two-light window in the east wall of the transept is apparently earlier than the east window of the chancel, there can be no doubt that the transept was built subsequently to the chancel. The former is constructed of ashlar blocks of granite; the latter of rubble. The transept, like that at St. Levan [g], is separated from the nave by two arches; the capitals of the piers having angels bearing shields. Two brackets project from the north wall.

East Window of Transept, St. Wendron.

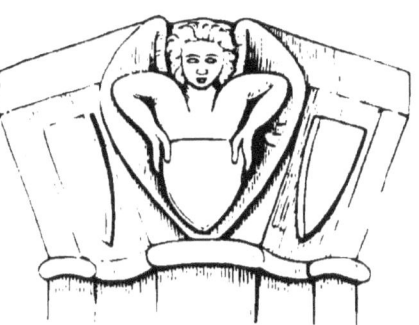

Capital of Transept Pier, St. Wendron.

The north window is Perpendicular with three lights, and of the same design as the east window of

[g] See above, p. 18.

the aisle of St. Antony[h]; it has, however, no hood-moulding.

The nave and aisle are divided by an arcade of five four-centred arches, with piers of late Decorated section. The westernmost capital is of similar design to those on the side piers separating transept from nave—a crowned angel dressed in a tunic and with arms extended holding a shield in each hand: the capitals of the remaining piers are represented by the annexed cut, and a section of the base mouldings is also given.

There is but one small two-light window on the north side of the nave; it resembles the window in St. Madron's tower [i].

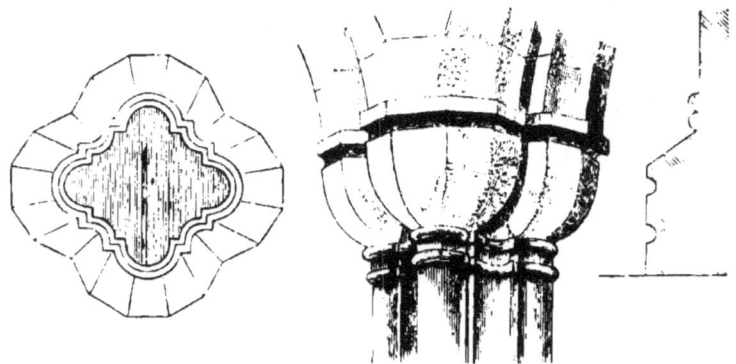

Section, Capital, and Base Mouldings of Aisle Piers, St. Wendron.

On the south side of the aisle are four windows; that west of the porch having tracery somewhat like

[h] See above, p. 80. [i] See above, p. 29.

the east window of the chancel. The other windows are also of Decorated character. The east window consists of three lights without tracery; it has, however, deeply moulded jambs, and the section of the hood-moulding is remarkable. The same moulding occurs over other windows of the aisle.

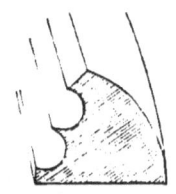

Section of Hood-moulding of Aisle Windows, St. Wendron.

The piscina in the south-east corner of the aisle is of unusual formation.

The font (see opposite), standing near the western end of the aisle, has the inwardly curved stem with slender shafts attached, and octagonal bowl, like others of the district previously noticed; the four sides

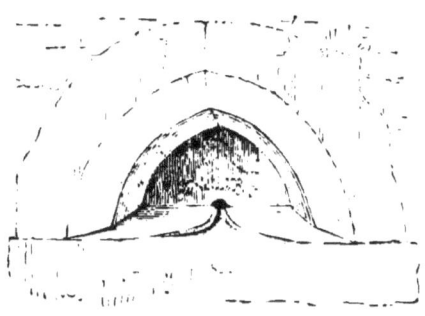

Piscina in Aisle, St. Wendron.

are ornamented with quatrefoils, and the material out of which the font is formed appears to be Caen stone.

The tower must be classed with the later parts of the building; it consists of three stages, is battlemented and pinnacled; and an unusual feature in construction for this part of the world is, that the buttresses are placed at the angles diagonally to the sides. Plain set-offs mark the stages, and each stage recedes to the parapet, which slightly projects. The cappings of the buttresses, though now much weather-worn, were effective in design, and shew how

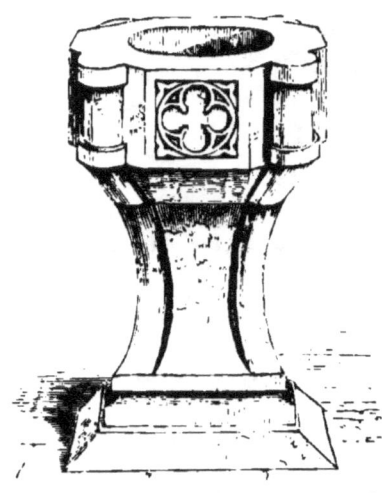

Font, St. Wendron.

Capping of Tower Buttresses, St. Wendron.

the old builders struggled with an obdurate material, (for the tower is of granite,) and sought by simple chamfering to give change of line and variety of form. There are four belfry windows, each of two lights, in the uppermost stage. The large west window is decidedly Perpendicular. The doorway has a plain chamfer. At the junction of the tower with the aisle there is a block of solid masonry carried up to the first set-off of the buttress. The object of this is not apparent.

The following quaint belfry rhyme is retained on the wall of the tower:—

> "We ring the quick to church, the dead to grave,
> Good is our use, such useage let us have.

> Who swears, or curse, or in a furious mood
> Quarels, or striks, altho he draws no blood,
> Who wears a hat, or spurs, or turns a bell,
> Or by unskilfull handling mars a peall,
> Let him pay sixpence for each single crime,
> Twill make him cautious gainst another time."

The porch is the latest part of the whole structure; like that at St. Burian, it has double buttresses at the angles and is battlemented. The buttresses are finished with pinnacles crocketed and finialed. The buttress cappings appear to be copied from those of the tower.

The church contains two or three monuments of interest. On the chancel floor are two brasses; one bears no inscription, but has the effigies of a man and woman. The other is much larger and is thus inscribed:—

"Hic jacet Magister Warinus Penhallinyk, in Decretis Baccalaureus, quondam Prebendarius Ecclesiæ Collegiatæ de Glasneth, necnon Rector Ecclesiæ Parochialis[k] Sancti Justi[l], et Vicarius Ecclesiarum Parochialium[m] Sanctarum Wendronæ et Stedianæ ; qui obiit nono die mensis Aprilis, Anno Domini millesimo quingentesimo trigesimo quinto : Cujus animæ propicietur Deus. Amen."

The figure of the priest has unfortunately lost its head (see opposite page).

Of more interest than these is a stone forming the step of the north door of the nave, now leading into the vestry. Its present is certainly not its original position, and there can be little doubt that it existed

---

[k] Spelt perochialis. [l] St. Just in Roseland.
[m] Spelt perochialium.

long before the building of the nave. It bears simply an incised Latin cross and circle, and may be a most

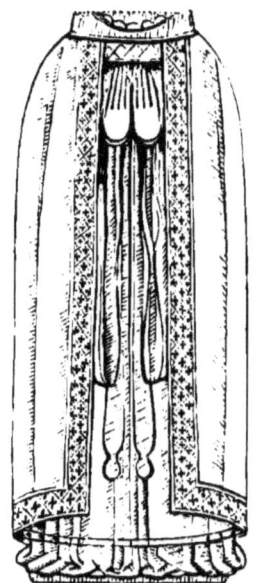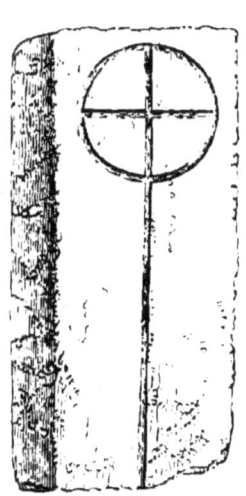

Brass of Warin Penhallinyk, and Incised Stone, St. Wendron.

early Christian monument. It measures in length 4 ft. 1 in., in breadth 1 ft. 8 in., and is 7 in. thick. A portion of the length has been broken off to make it fit into the breadth of the doorway.

Though in some instances the Decorated work of St. Wendron much resembles the work of the same period at St. Mawgan, still the church has many distinct features from those of other churches of the neighbourhood, especially in the arrangement of the chancel, and the superiority of its piers with their capitals and bases; some of the windows are also very good; and because it contains much Decorated work, in a country abounding with inferior Perpendicular, is the building chiefly noticeable.

The chancel has been restored by the Rev. G. B. Boraston, the vicar, within the last few years.

Of the patron saint nothing is known. In the *Valor Ecclesiasticus*, 1536, the name is spelt "Gwendrone." Dr. Oliver in his *Monasticon* says that the church is dedicated to St. Wendrona, but does not give the date of dedication. He adds that there was a chapel at Merthen Park in this parish, dedicated to St. Decumanus, which was licensed on the 18th of August, 1427. Also that the great tithes were appropriated to the abbey of "Rewley, regalis loci, juxta Oxon[n]."

Some remains of the chapel, and a tall round-headed cross in good preservation, still exist at Merthen.

VII. ST. BREAGE—ST. GERMOE—ST. PERRAN-UTHNOE.

BREACA, a lady of rank, and Germoe, a king, belonged to that large company of Irish missionaries which, according to the tradition, landed, some time in the fifth century, at Riviere, at the mouth of the Hayle. Several of these saints were slain, says Dr. Borlase, near where they came ashore, by Theodoric, a heathen king of Cornwall. Dr. Whitaker, on the

---

[n] Bp. Stapledon's Register, fol. 180.

other hand, contends that this king was a Christian, that a few of the party were killed only, through mistake, and that as soon as Theodoric became aware of the nature of their holy mission he treated them with great hospitality, and permitted them to go where they would.

> "Germoe mather
> Breaga lavethes."
> i.e. "Germoe a king
> Breage a midwife,"

is an old Cornish distich which some have attempted to explain in a spiritual sense. However this may be, it seems that St. Breaca and St. Germoe crossed from Riviere to the southern coast[o], where the former caused a church to be built, and St. Germoe made his abode at a short distance.

ST. BREAGE is the mother church of St. Germoe, St. Cury, and St. Gunwalloe. The parish of Sithney intervenes between St. Breage and St. Gunwalloe, but St. Germoe adjoins St. Breage on the west and is separated from St. Perran-uthnoe only by a narrow strip of the parish of St. Hilary, which in a curious manner runs down to the sea, apparently just to claim the prominent headland known as Cudden Point. St. Germoe does not extend to the sea, for all the line of coast, excepting Cudden Point, from Maendu,

[o] Dr. Whitaker seriously suggests that St. Breaca came to this spot to reform wreckers! And strange to say, there are still to be found a few persons so utterly ignorant in regard to their own country as to believe that wrecking is even now practised in Cornwall!

which is a little eastward of St. Michael's Mount, to Porthleven, is included in the parishes of St. Perran-uthnoe and St. Breage. A glance at the map will shew how strangely this group of parishes is divided.

Starting either from Helston or Penzance it would be possible, with tolerable ease, to visit in one day the three churches which form the subject of this paper. If not pressed for time a pleasant excursion might be made by leaving Penzance and proceeding direct to St. Perran-uthnoe Church, thence down to Perran Sands, and across Cudden Point, just beyond which is Prussia Cove with a coast-guard station and a few fishermen's houses. Then on to the fine stretch of beach called Pra Sands. About a quarter of a mile from the shore stands Pengerswick Castle, built in the early part of the sixteenth century, and was the residence of the Militons. One of this family, Job Militon, was governor of St. Michael's Mount in the time of Edward VI. The greater part of the building has long ago fallen into decay, but a three-storied and battlemented tower remains in tolerable preservation. An upper room adjoining the tower had panelled walls, each panel containing a rude painting with a legend in verse beneath [p].

[p] The following, entitled "Perseverance," affords a good example of these verses :—

"What thing is harder than the rock
  What softer is than water cleere?
Yet wyll the same, with often droppe,
  The hard rock perce, as doth a spere;

Following along the coast, the next remarkable place is Trewavas Head, where a detached mass of granite called the "Bishop Rock" assumes the form of a colossal figure with its back to the sea, and with clasped hands resting on a lectern, whilst the robe trails down the cliff side. It does not require the aid of imagination to trace in this naturally formed figure the striking resemblance to a kneeling monk, and it is much superior to many similarly situated rocks on the coast to which names have been given for their supposed likeness to familiar things or remarkable personages [q].

Referring to this locality, Mr. W. J. Henwood says:—

"The wild romantic character of the coast is inferior to nothing of the kind in Cornwall; and Wheal Trewavas [r], which has its engines perched on the cliffs, and its workings beneath the sea, is quite as picturesque as Botallack or Levant in the St. Just district [s]."

Even so, nothing so hard to attayne,
But may be hadd with labour and payne."

Other lines refer to certain abuses of the time of Henry VIII., probably strictures on that monarch himself.

[q] The Rev. C. A. Johns has figured the Bishop Rock in his instructive "Week at the Lizard."

[r] Wheal Vor, also in this parish, has been in its time one of the richest mines in Cornwall:—"The present working of Wheal Vor has been continued about eighteen years, and in that time about £1,240,000 worth of tin has been raised, of which I believe that more than £100,000 has been profit to the adventurers."—*W. J. Henwood, F.R.S., F.G.S., in Trans. Geological Society of Cornwall*, vol. v. 1843.

[s] *Trans. Geological Society of Cornwall*, vol. v.

St. Breage Church is little more than two miles from the coast, and to succeed in the tour of inspection of the three churches it would now be necessary to proceed to the church town, and thence to St. Germoe.

Before describing the church it may be worth while to refer to a few other objects in St. Breage. In this parish are two hills called Godolphin and Tregoning, which are conspicuous from all the shores of Mount's Bay. At the foot of the former stands the old mansion-house, (a quadrangular building of the time of Queen Elizabeth,) of the noble family of Godolphin. The meaning of the word Godolphin has not been satisfactorily explained, and it appears that the family took a portion of the word literally, and adopted a dolphin for their crest, as may be seen on the old helmets in St Breage Church.

Helmet, St. Breage.

On the summit of Tregoning Hill are the remains of a large fort, or as it is termed in Cornwall, a "hill-castle." This appears to have been of great strength, and was one of the largest structures of the kind in Cornwall. The hill was formerly called Pencairn, and Leland refers to the castle as Cair Kenin, *alias* Gonyn and Conin.

It was to this hill of Pencairn that St. Breaca first came after leaving Riviere, and, says Leland, "*ædificavit eccl. in Trenewith et Talmeneth.*" The ancient name of the parish was Pembro, and the place called Trenewith is some distance from the site of the present church, which stands on rising ground adjoining the high-road leading from Helston to Penzance.

The church possesses no architectural features of particular interest; it consists of a chancel and nave, with western tower, north and south aisles, each with a small transeptal projection, probably constructed as chapels for, and at the cost of, important families of the locality. The wooden roof of the north transept has some well-carved bosses. The south aisle has a porch of the same local character as those of St. Burian and St. Wendron previously described.

The piers separating the aisles from the nave are of the usual type, consisting of four rounded and four cavetto mouldings; the cavettos, however, are broader than usual. The capitals also resemble those found in other Perpendicular churches in western Cornwall. Indeed, the church throughout is of the fifteenth century; all traces of earlier work, if any exist, being obscured by later additions and alterations. The tower

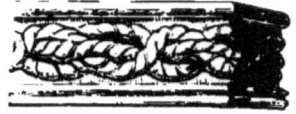

Capitals, St. Breage.

is so nearly like that of St. Germoe that the description to be given of the latter will serve for both. There is considerable difference, however, between the tower-arches. At St. Breage the arch is panelled, of lofty proportions, and is perhaps the finest Perpendicular arch to be found in any of the churches of the district.

A few years ago the head of a cross was discovered buried in the churchyard; it is similar in form to others existing in churchyards in Cornwall, is evidently much older than the present church, and may be contemporaneous with the original fabric. As at St. Burian, this cross has lost its shaft.

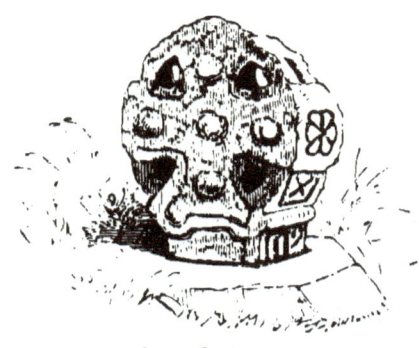

Cross, St. Breage.

In the taxation of Pope Nicholas IV., (A.D. 1288-91,) the entry is as follows:—

"Ecclesia Sanctæ Breacæ. Taxatio £16; Decima £1 12s.; Vicaria ejusdem £1 6s. 8d."

ST. GERMOE at one time appears to have been a Decorated cruciform church; the north transept having been superseded by a fifteenth-century aisle, to which a shallow transeptal projection was added, as at St. Breage and elsewhere.

The south transept, wall of nave, and porch, are all that remain of the Decorated work, and these present interesting and remarkable features, differing materially from other churches of the district. In

St. Germoe Church.

most of the early transeptal churches the porch either adjoins or is very near the transept, as if later additions; here, however, the porch is 11 ft. from the transept, and between the two, in the wall of the nave, is a peculiar Decorated square window of three ogee-headed lights with quatrefoils in the head. The south window of the transept was apparently of the same design, but the quatrefoils have been removed and the space between the points of the three lights and the square hoodmould occupied by solid masonry. This accounts for the great height of the mould above the lights. In the east wall of the transept is a window of two ogee-headed lights.

There does not appear to have been an oblique wall at the junction with the chancel, but, at the angle, mouldings are carried up to the height of seven feet, where they sprung into a diagonal arch, of which only twelve or thirteen inches remain. This probably formed the narrow passage at the end of the screen, and led from the chancel to the transept. If such were the case, it shews that the primary object of this peculiar construction was rather to afford means of communication than for the purpose of a hagioscope, though we have seen they are in several instances combined. At St. Perran-uthnoe another variation of the prevailing plan will be noticed. The transept is divided from the nave by a single pier rising from a rude block of stone, between two and three feet high before the moulding commences, and supporting a square beam of oak, extending across the breadth of the transept. The capital and mouldings of this pier are similar to those between nave and aisle at St. Wendron[1]. A moulded corbel projects from the west wall of the transept, and probably supported an earlier roof.

The inner and outer doorways of the porch have deep mouldings of a superior character. The pretty

[1] See above, p. 103

gable cross, and grotesquely sculptured gable corbels, are also features of rare occurrence; indeed they may be said to be unique in West Cornwall.

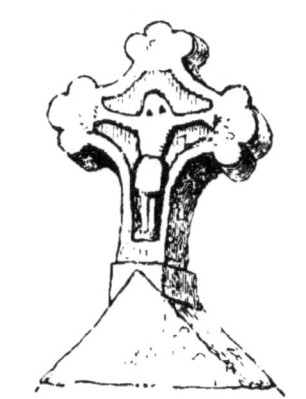

Gable Cross of Porch, St. Germoe.

The tower at the west end of the nave is Perpendicular, of three stages, unbuttressed. Plain set-offs mark the stages, each receding a little to the parapet. More labour than usual has been bestowed on the upper part. The battlements are certainly of a simple description, but the pinnacles vary from the general type; each springs from an angel, and consists of a square, panelled shaft, battlemented, crocketed above, and capped by a flat square finial, on

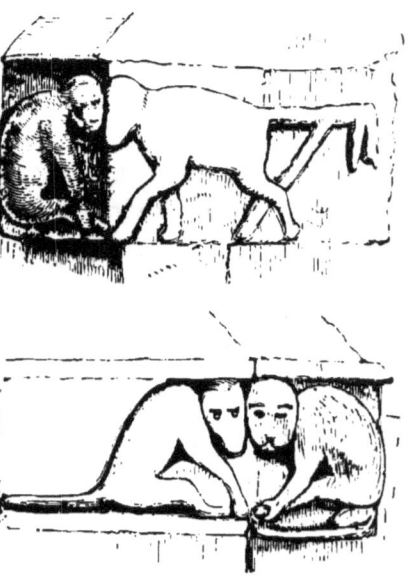

Gable Corbels of Porch, St. Germoe.

which a cross is placed. At the foot of the parapet are grotesquely sculptured gargoyles.

The four belfry windows are each of three lights, with two quatrefoils in the head. A well-moulded plinth is carried around the base, and about 2 ft. above it a bold stringcourse. The western doorway consists of a four-centred arch under a square hoodmould, with square terminations, on which oak-leaves are sculptured.

The tower-arch has ogee mouldings.

There are three bells, all dated 1753, and with the same founder's mark, a bell. Two have the founder's initials, "A. R.," whilst the third is inscribed,—

"Abel Rudhall
Cast us all."

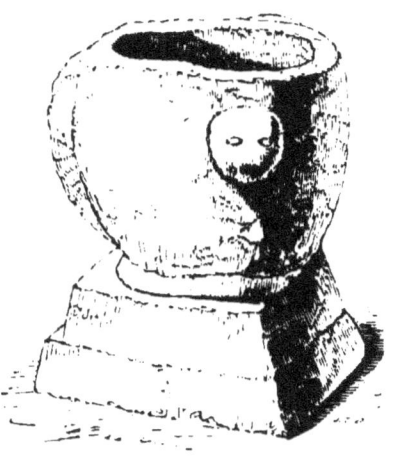

Font, St. Germoe.

Although the church may have existed as a Decorated cross church, the font is certainly of earlier date, and is perhaps one of the most ancient fonts in Cornwall. It is rudely and irregularly formed, and has on opposite sides two heads carved in bold relief, whilst just between them is a curious projection of a fish-like form, extending the whole depth of the bowl.

On the floor lies the fragment of a Norman font, which may have belonged to some chapel in the neighbourhood.

The chancel has been rebuilt.

St. Germoe's Chair.

At the north-east angle of the churchyard is a curious structure, popularly known as "St. Germoe's Chair," or, "King Germoe's Throne." Its form is oblong, measuring, internally, 3 ft. 6 in. by 6 ft. 3 in. The front is formed by two arches, each 6 ft. high, and supported on round pillars. At the back is a seat, 1 ft. 4 in. high, extending the whole length of the building, and divided into three equal compartments by two shafts, which serve as supports for three arches; those on the sides being 3 ft. 8 in. high, whilst the centre one rises 4 in. higher, and has on its apex a sculptured head of the Blessed Virgin wearing a crown. A head also projects from the outside of the front wall.

These sedilia do not appear to have been removed from elsewhere, but to occupy their original position. The situation commands a view of the greater part of the churchyard, and it is possible the structure was erected for the convenience of priests in churchyard ceremonies. The work is of early character.

Referring to St. Germoe's Church, Leland says, "his tumbe is yet scene ther." He also speaks of "St. Germoke's Chair in the Chirch-yard," and of "St. Germoke's Welle a little without the Chirch-yard." No traces of the latter remain, but a small stream runs just by the southern entrance to the churchyard, and here the well may have stood.

ST. PIRAN, one of the most noted saints of Ireland, came into Cornwall in the early part of the fifth century. That he was highly esteemed amongst the Cornish is shewn by the fact that four parish churches in the county bear his name—Perran-zabuloe, Perran-arworthal, Perran-uthnoe [u], and St. Kevern or Pieran, called Lanachebran in Domesday. There is also

---

[u] In the taxation of Pope Nicholas, St. Piran-uthnoe is entered "Ecclesia de Lanudno."

the well of St. Perran on the northern shores of Perran-zabuloe.

The church of St. Perran-uthnoe is situated near the coast, opposite St. Michael's Mount. It seems probable that the site was, at an early date, occupied by an ecclesiastical edifice, though there are few remains of an ancient character in the existing building.

Judging from the external appearance of the walls, the oldest part is the transept, which has the hagioscopic passage at the junction with the chancel resembling those in the churches of the Lizard district. The oblique wall, however, forms a much less angle; it is very rudely constructed, and at the height of eighteen inches from the ground projects a little from the foundation. One of the lower stones has marks of incised decoration of a very primitive character, and probably formed part of a much earlier structure.

This oblique wall has no window as in the other examples, but adjoining it in the eastern wall of the transept may be seen, internally, an obtusely pointed arch, two feet in breadth, and forming a recess, which now extends only to the springing of the arch, though there are traces that it once reached the floor, and was either a narrow aperture through, or a shallow recess 4 ft. 8 in. high in, the wall. Externally, the masonry has been much disturbed, and the upper portion, at least, appears to have been pierced through.

Whether this peculiar arrangement is any way analogous to certain provisions made for the benefit of what are termed Cagots, referred to by Mr. Wright, may be worthy of consideration. In this maritime part of the country, and so near St. Michael's Mount, it is not unlikely that many individuals, from whom the inhabitants of the country would keep apart, might be brought into the neighbourhood.

In plan, the church is much the same as others already noticed. In addition to the chancel (recently rebuilt) and south transept, it has nave with western tower and south porch, and a north aisle. There is a space of 5 ft. between the transept and the porch, and in the intervening wall of the nave a small ugly modern sash window, the only window, in fact, in the nave. The transept window is of like character. A Perpendicular window of three lights occupies the west end of the aisle; those in the north wall, each of two lights, are of Debased character.

The piers between nave and aisle are of rather an unusual section; the capitals consist of a series of plain chamfers.

As usual, the tower is Perpendicular, of three stages, battlemented and pinnacled, with four belfry lights, a western window and doorway under a square hoodmould. The corbels of the tower-arch are worthy of notice, as varying from the ordinary type. One only is finished, as shewn by the woodcut, the other being inserted as a plain pentagonal block, intended probably to have been subsequently worked on.

The font, of granite, is square, with one side panelled, and may be of early date.

The hoodmould terminations of the south door are

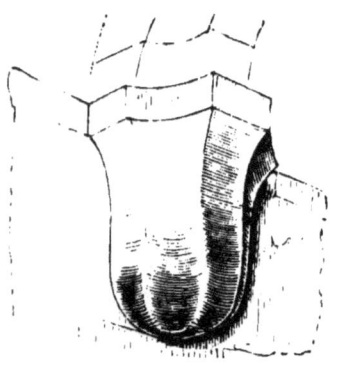

Corbel, Tower-arch, St. Perran-uthnoe.

Keystone of South Doorway, and Figure of St. James the Great, St. Perran-uthnoe.

sculptured heads: one of a bishop. The keystone is a head with a lolling tongue, over which, built into the wall, is a piece of granite, having a sculptured figure of St. James the Great with his staff and book. Some interest may be attached to this stone because we have pretty sure knowledge of its date; it affords, therefore, an example of the capabilities of the workmen in this neighbourhood at a certain period. In the first instance, it is rare to find at all, in West Cornwall churches, representations of particular saints; what little sculpture exists is mostly of a general character, so there must have been some reason why St. James was specially selected.

It is said, and there can be little doubt on the subject, that this stone was brought from the ruins of a chapel at the village of Goldsithney, in this parish. Documentary evidence proves the existence of such a chapel, and Dr. Oliver states in his *Monasticon* that St. James's Chapel at Goldsithney was licensed July 12, 1450. Now, as pilgrimages were made to St. Michael's Mount, it is very easy to conceive that a chapel would have been erected at that spot

"Where the great vision of the guarded Mount"

first burst on the gaze of the weary, yet gladdened, travellers. When the noble bay was first seen spread out before them, and the strange sight of the monastery on the island rock came into view, the pilgrimage might have been considered as almost concluded; and here, in the chapel of the very patron of pilgrims, were thanks given for escapes from all dangers, and for protection granted on the way.

VIII. ST. GULVAL — ST. LUDGVAN — ST. ERTH — LELANT—ST. GWINEAR—ST. GWITHIAN.

ST. GULVAL (or St. GUDWALL) CHURCH, embosomed in foliage, is pleasantly situated about a mile from Penzance, on the northern shore of Mount's Bay. It has chancel, nave with transept and western tower, south aisle and porch. On the south side of the chancel are sedile and piscina, and in the north wall a credence, all having arches of Decorated character; those of the sedile and credence being cinquefoiled, the piscina trefoiled.

The transept, as at St. Levan[x], is divided from the nave by two arches with plain octagonal piers.

A small well-sculptured corbel-head projects from the spandril between the second and third arches of the nave, and on the moulding of the third arch are traces of ancient painting; the figure remaining looks like the termination of a crocketed and finialed canopy, with a lettered scroll on either side.

Credence, St. Gulval.

The tower, a very plain granite structure, has three stages carried up on nearly the same plane to the parapet, which overhangs, with a hollow mould; and at the angles immediately under the parapet are sculptured figures, probably intended for the four Evangelists.

The belfry windows, each of three lights, have a kind of geometrical tracery without cusps. The mouldings of the

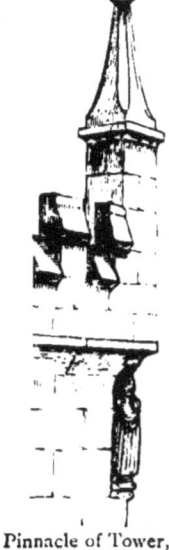
Pinnacle of Tower, St. Gulval.

[x] See above, p. 18.

western doorway consist of three rounds and two cavettos; and the plinth mouldings (a round and chamfer), which in other towers of the district stop at the springings of the arch, are here continued boldly as a hoodmould over the doorway.

The staircase is contained in the thickness of the north wall, with an entrance from without; an inner doorway is blocked up. The tower-arch differs from any other previously noticed, being a plain soffit-arch with chamfered imposts, and underneath (as if an afterthought) responds with a moulded arch.

The very simplicity of the tower renders it worthy of notice. There are three bells of late date; one bears the following :—

"ILE . RING . ALLWAYS . MY . MAKERS . PRAYES. 1675."

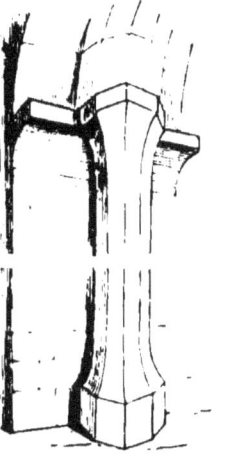

Tower-arch, St. Gulval.

Between each word is stamped the head of Charles II., with the superscription, CAROLUS II. DEO GRATIA, like a coin of the period, and about the size of a shilling.

The general form of the font resembles that at St. Burian,[7] having a pedestal consisting of three-quarter rounds at the angles, with a cavetto between

---

[7] See above, p. 6.

each. At one angle of the bowl is an angel; the others have shields curiously sculptured.

Shields on Font, St. Gulval.

This church was reseated and partially restored in 1857; and some good stained glass memorial windows have recently been inserted.

A curious old cross stands in the south-eastern corner of the churchyard [2].

The church of ST. LUDGVAN, ST. LUDOWANUS, occupies a commanding station two miles eastward of St. Gulval. No finer view of Mount's Bay can be had than from the roof of the tower. The church is of some interest to Cornishmen, as it contains the monument of Dr. Borlase, the eminent county antiquary, and for many years Rector of the parish. In this parish also was Sir Humphry Davy born, and there is a tablet in the church to the memory of the father and mother of the great philosopher.

Architecturally, the church is of little interest; it has chancel, nave with western tower, and north and south aisles, with a south porch.

[2] See "Ancient Crosses, &c., in West Cornwall," p. 51.

The bowl of the font appears to be the sole relic of earlier work; it has a cable moulding, scolloped sides, and a rude tooth-ornament above. Its date is probably transition from Norman to Early English [a].

The tower is fully developed, of three stages buttressed on square at the angles; the belfry lights resemble those at St. Gulval; and the parapet, pinnacles, and gurgoyles are like those at St. Germoe [b]. The tower-arch is panelled.

Rudely formed figures of the Crucifixion, with St. Andrew and other saints, are inlaid with coloured woods in the panels of the pulpit.

Window, North Aisle, St. Erth.

ST. ERTH CHURCH is worthy of notice as possessing very early and good Perpendicular work. The

[a] See "Week at the Land's End," p. 226. [b] See above, p 115.

chancel appears to have been built in the latter part of the fourteenth century, during the Transition period, and has a good window of that date. The north aisle east window (see opposite), Perpendicular, is divided into three lights, and has a hoodmoulding, much decayed, with capped heads as terminations. The south aisle window is of five lights and later. The east walls of the aisles are flush with the wall of the chancel.

The porch is buttressed, has panelled jambs to the outer door, and over its apex a rather richly carved canopied niche, now occupied by a sundial.

The tower has three stages of the ordinary Cornish type; the belfry windows are early Perpendicular. At the angles of the uppermost stringcourse are grotesque figures of dogs and other animals; the only instance of this kind of decoration in West Cornwall. The pinnacles are of later date.

Stringcourse, Tower, St. Erth.

This church contains a cenotaph to the memory of Davies Gilbert, President of the Royal Society, and author of a "Parochial History of the County of Cornwall."

LELANT CHURCH is built among the sandbanks which line the southern shore of St. Ives Bay. Its plan closely resembles that of St. Erth, having chancel and nave with north and south aisles to both, with south porch and western tower; and is interesting chiefly for its Norman remains, consisting of an

K

entire arch, pier, and half-pier, forming the second bay on the north side of the nave.

The springing of a second arch to the east is to be seen on the south side. The capitals are scolloped, and the base has simply a round and chamfer on a square plinth. Westward of the Norman work is an acutely-pointed arch of the thirteenth century, of plain masonry without mouldings.

The rest of the church is Perpendicular. The porch is like that at St. Erth, and has a niche for a stoup, the vessel itself being removed.

Capital and Base of Norman Pier, Lelant.

Those who are curious in such matters will find quaint inscriptions on the tablets against the west wall of the south aisle.

There is some fair modern glass in this church.

Outside the western entrance is a round-headed cross, and another, having St. Andrew's cross in bold relief, stands within the churchyard.

The patron saint is St. Ewinus.

ST. GWINEAR. This church stands on high ground about three miles from Hayle. Its plan is rendered peculiar by the addition of a chapel 32 ft. long to the side of the north aisle. It was probably built by some lord of an estate in the parish; and that it was for the separate use of a family would seem to be shewn by the curious entrance at the west end, the north-east corner of the porch having been cut away for the purpose of giving access to the door

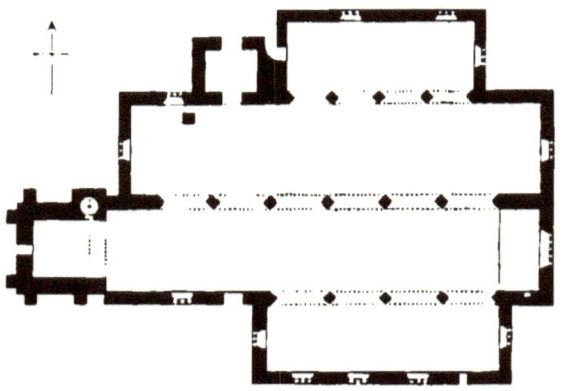

Plan of St. Gwinear Church.

of the chapel. An addition of this kind frequently assumes, in Cornwall, the form of a small transeptal projection. Here, however, it has nearly the proportions of an aisle, being divided from the north aisle by four arches with octagonal piers; the capitals having angels holding shields. One shield not so supported has the figure of a deer, or stag,—perhaps the arms of the person who raised the structure. The work is late, probably of the sixteenth century.

It is uncertain what was the original plan of this church. The west wall of the south aisle is older than that on the south; possibly it was the west side of a transept contemporaneous with the existing chancel, which is of good early Decorated date. The east window is of five lights, with mullions carried on through the head and simply intersecting each other. A portion of the upper part of the tracery

Chancel Window, St. Gwinear.

having fallen away, the vacant space has been built up. The splay-arch has detached shafts, with heads as capitals. This window is a valuable example of the period, and of a type seldom met with in Cornwall[c].

The piscina in the south wall is of the same date;

[c] The east window of Lesnewth Church, in Cornwall, is a fine example of this type.

its chamfer-stops are curious and unusual in these parts.

The nave and aisles are late Perpendicular, of much the same character as other churches in the district previously noticed. It is, however, rare to find the porch on the north side. The south doorway has been blocked up. Both north and south doorways have the Tudor rose carved in the spandrils. Built into the wall of the porch are two beak-heads of Norman date, indicating that an earlier structure once occupied the site; and two grotesque heads joined together

Piscina, St. Gwinear.

Beak-head, Porch, St. Gwinear.

Corbel-heads, Tower, St. Gwinear.

are built into the western wall of the tower about 10 ft. from the ground, and north of the doorway. Another anciently sculptured head is inserted in the west wall of the tower; all, undoubtedly, relics of the previous church.

The tower is of three stages, doubly buttressed at the angles, and has the staircase on the north side contained in a square turret rising above the parapet, and battlemented and pinnacled. At the base the staircase is lighted with a trefoil, and above by square slits. The lower stages have windows of Decorated character, resembling those at St. Madron[d]. The upper windows are Perpendicular, each of three lights. The tower was not finished in the year 1441, for we learn from Dr. Oliver's *Monasticon* that "Michael L'Archdekne, treasurer of Exeter Cathedral, left by will, dated Jan. 5, 1441, forty shillings towards the building of the tower, or purchase of bells *Ecclesie Sancti Wynneri.*" It was probably then in progress.

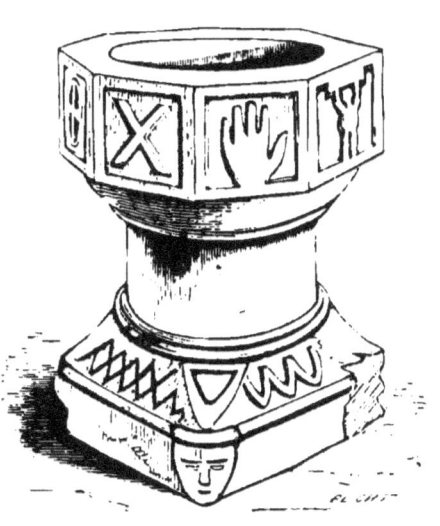

Font, St. Gwinear.

The bowl of the font is octagonal, dated 1727, and has each face carved, the devices being — a heart, a hand, St. Andrew's cross, figure of our Lord on a Tau cross,

[d] See above, p. 29.

head with nimbus, &c. The pedestal and base are of early date; on the splay of the latter is a lozenge and scollop pattern; and at each corner was a projecting head, one of which still remains. The bowl may be sculptured in imitation of an older one.

Fragments of the old carved benchends and wood-work remain. The frequent repetition of a hand is remarkable: in one instance it is pierced and has a crown over it, representing one of the five sacred wounds.

Symbol of Sacred Wound, St. Gwinear.

Dr. Oliver, under the signature "Curiosus," published in a local paper some interesting notes relating to this church and its vicars. It appears that "Gilbert de Clare, Earl of Gloucester and Hertford, as chief lord of the manor, at the instance of Walter Stapledon, Bishop of Exeter, authorized by his deed, dated Westminster, May 24, 1311, the grant of an acre of land in the manor of *Draynet*, now called Drannock, with the advowson of the church *Sancti Wynneri*, to Sir Richard Stapledon in aid of, and for the maintenance of, twelve scholars in the University of Oxford."

The Doctor says that before its annexation to Exeter College he had met with but a single Rector, viz. "Robert Fitz-Robert, whom Bishop Bronescombe admitted on Jan. 12, 1261, 'ad Ecclesiam Sancti

Winneri vacantem,' on the presentation of Jane 'Domine de Campo Arnulpho,' or Champernoun."

The church is dedicated to St. Winnerus; and in a note to the paper from which the preceding extracts are taken, Dr. Oliver adds, "For any acts or particulars of this saint I have hitherto searched in vain."

St. Gwithian (or St. Gothian) Church, on the eastern shore of St. Ives Bay, as it now stands has chancel, nave with western tower, north transept, and south aisle with porch. The original building was evidently cruciform, and of Early English date.

Transept, St. Gwithian.

The transept of this period remains, and its arch is of a kind not usually found in West Cornwall.

There are also traces of a chancel-arch, a very rare feature in the county: the removal of the south transept for the aisle must have caused its fall.

The recess in the east wall of the transept was possibly an aumbry: there was of course an altar here; and the piscina may be hid beneath the plastering.

The tower is good Perpendicular, earlier than the aisle; it has three stages, with parapet and pinnacles like those at St. Germoe. There are angels at the angles, but no gargoyles.

The font consists of a late square bowl placed on an early round shaft.

In the year 1782 the chancel was rebuilt; and a good Decorated stained glass window of three lights has been inserted by the present Rector, the Rev. Frederick Hockin.

In the churchyard stands a round-headed cross, having a Greek cross, with a boss on its centre in relief, within the circle.

Among the sand-banks about a quarter of a mile from the church are the ruins of the ancient oratory of St. Gothian. At the time of its discovery, about thirty-five years ago, it was totally buried beneath a turf-clad mound. Externally, the sand is still level with the tops of the walls, which vary from 5 to 7 ft. in height. The length of the building, internally, is 48 ft. 11 in.; of this the chancel occupies 17 ft. 1 in., and is 12 ft. 2 in. wide. The nave,

31 ft. 10 in. in length, measures 14 ft. 4 in. in breadth at the east end, but at the west end is 6 in. narrower.

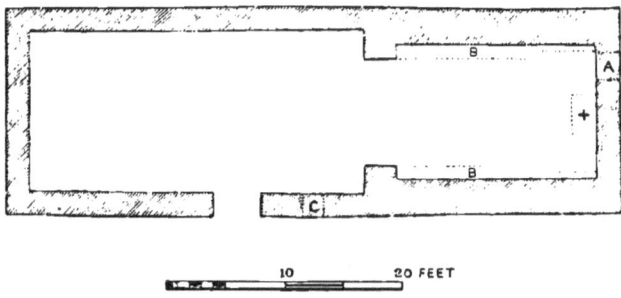

Plan of St. Gothian's Oratory.

The doorway is in the south wall of the nave, 9 ft. from the chancel. There appears to have been a priest's doorway at A in the plan, and at C a small window. On examining the foundations beneath the present covering of sand, traces of stone benches (BB) were discovered along the chancel and sacrarium. There was also an altar of masonry—pulled down when the owner of the land turned the oratory into a cowshed!

Three small square holes in the western wall were probably left for putlogs.

The plan of this little structure resembles that of the famed oratory of St. Piran: both were similarly situated, and were discovered under like circumstances, for the eastern side of St. Ives Bay, as well as the coast at Perranzabuloe, is overwhelmed with sand. It has been conjectured that when St. Piran's

Oratory was built, the sand had not reached the spot. Such, however, was the case, the foundations being laid on the sand. The fact of these buildings being found buried does not afford any clue to their age, for the sands have been continually shifting; and so lately as a hundred years ago the house of the barton of Upton, in the parish of St. Gwithian, was overwhelmed, and the family had to escape by the windows. In 1808 a drift disclosed the house still standing. We have, therefore, no other means of judging as to the period when those structures were raised but by the character of the work, and this seems to indicate an early date. From the absence of all mouldings, and from the rudeness of

Doorway of St. Gothian's Oratory.

the construction of St. Gothian's Oratory, it would appear to be of higher antiquity than that of St. Piran. It will be remembered that the latter possessed a doorway with a kind of zigzag moulding, and sculptured heads at the springings and keystone of the arch [e]. At St. Gothian's Oratory the stones, consisting of slate, quartz, and sandstone, seem to have been built in just as they came to hand. A large piece of sandstone in the eastern jamb of the doorway may, perhaps, have been worked into form; it is the same kind of stone as that referred to as existing in early work at St. Levan, St. Burian, and Landewednack.

No cement of any sort is used in the masonry. At St. Piran's, however, the walls at the back of the benches are plastered with unwashed china-clay, none of which could have been procured within a distance of ten or twelve miles [f].

These oratories were of greater dimensions, but are certainly to be classed with other structures of like character, remains of which are to be found on different parts of the Cornish coast, more frequently in the Land's End district. In plan they are simply parallelograms, with some distinguishing mark dividing the altar platform, and a stone altar. No roofs remain. From their extreme simplicity, and the rudeness of the masonry, they are evidently of very early date; but for what special purpose constructed is uncertain. They may have been the oratories of holy men many centuries ago, and some

[e] These heads are now in the Museum of the Royal Institution of Cornwall at Truro.

[f] Ferruginous limestone occurs in several parts of the neighbouring cliffs, and it has been burnt for modern building purposes at Lower St. Colomb Porth, within five or six miles of the ancient oratory.

of them appear to have given a peculiar sanctity to the locality, marking the site and providing the dedication for a subsequent parochial church.

In the sand around both the oratories of St. Gothian and St. Piran numerous human skeletons were found, as if the spots had been specially selected as burial-places. At Porth Curnow, near St. Levan Church, on the southern coast of the Land's End district, are the remains of one of those ancient oratories or chapels. The courses of stone were built with some regularity. Two small openings in the west wall appear to have served as windows, and, like St. Piran's and St. Gothian's oratories, this little structure is situated near a rivulet; indeed, nearly all such buildings are so. But the remarkable peculiarity at Porth Curnow is that the chapel appears

Porth Curnow Chapel.

to have been built on an artificially raised mound; and about two or three yards from its western wall the present tenant of the estate found, a few years ago, in digging up the ground, a large sepulchral urn. Was the site, therefore, accidentally selected, or was it a spot greatly venerated, as the grave of some noted personage during the age of urn-burial, over which, on the introduction of Christianity, the little oratory was erected, that true worship might be offered there?

IX. ST. IVES—TOWEDNACK—ZENNOR—ST. HILARY —SITHNEY—ST. CROWAN—CAMBORNE.

ST. IVES.—This is a large church, consisting of chancel, nave with western tower, north and south aisles to both, with porch, and a side chapel [g] opening by an arcade of two into the eastern part of the south aisle. The east walls of the aisles and chapel are all flush with that of the chancel.

The chapel was added, but the other portions of the structure appear to have been built according to one design, without any additions or alterations, excepting those which were barbarously effected in almost every church during Puritanical times.

The roodloft staircase is at the north-west angle of the chapel. The roodscreen has been removed, but some of the carved oak benches remain.

One Ralph Clies, the master smith who superintended the smiths' work, is said to have made a present of a carved screen. The front panels of

---

[g] Connected with the Trenwith estate, and now commonly called the "Trenwith aisle."

a seat now in the chancel have shields bearing—
1. Hammer, pincers, nails, and horse-shoe; 2. Ham-

Shields on panels of seat, St. Ives.

mer and anvil; 3. A head; 4. A head; 5. Pair of bellows; 6. Ladle, trammers, and clefts. These are said to represent the smith's implements; and the figures 3 and 4 to be intended for Master Clies and his wife.

Each aisle has seven bays, with piers consisting of

Section of Pier, St. Ives. Pier-arch Moulding, St. Ives.

four shafts with intervening ogee mouldings; the arch-mouldings correspond.

The roofs are of the usual waggon form, but very handsome and perfect, elaborately carved, and with full-length figures of angels at the springings of the braces; these figures are continued all the way down the nave, and similar ones occur at St. Madron and a few other churches in Cornwall. In the chancel-roof only the braces and purlins are inter-

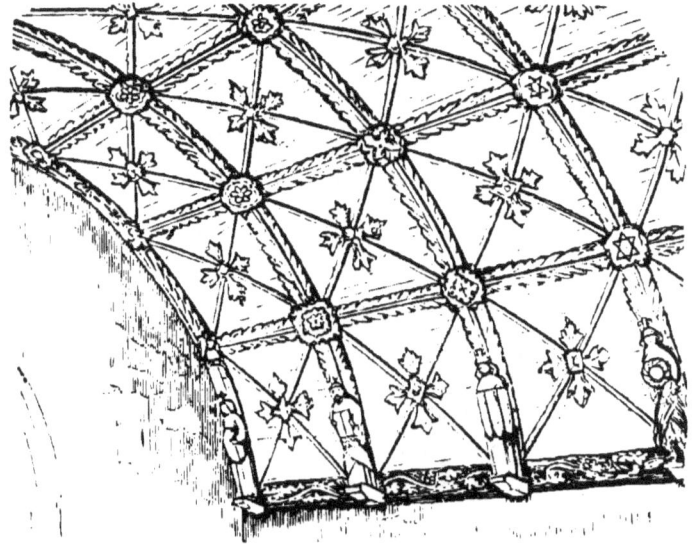

Chancel-roof, St. Ives.

sected diagonally by a raised and continuous moulding, giving a pretty net-like appearance. The suggestive vine pattern is carried along the wall-plate both in chancel and nave. Richly carved bosses are placed at the intersections of the diagonal lines and of the purlins and braces.

In the east wall of the north aisle and adjoining the chancel is an arched recess, with jambs resting on the floor, 4 ft. 2 in. high and 2 ft. 4 in. wide. It is too low for a doorway, and the exterior of the wall shews no indication of its being blocked up.

The tower, 119 ft. high, is of four stages, buttressed on square, has a battlemented parapet, and battlemented pinnacles resting on angels. The belfry windows, larger than usual, are each of three lights and transomed.

Several well-sculptured corbel-heads under the roof of the south chapel appear to be of earlier date than the wall into which they are built.

There is a very fine font, 3 ft. 10 in. high, apparently of the thirteenth century, but, as it is of

Font, St. Ives.

granite, may be a copy of a similar one of that date. On the bowl are four angels connected by bands, on one of which are, in raised early English characters, the words "Omnes baptizate gentes." Four dragons on the base symbolize the demons cast out by the power of baptism.

C. S. Gilbert, in his "History of Cornwall," quoting from the MSS. of a Mr. Hicks, who gleaned from the borough records of St. Ives, gives the following :—

"As it had pleased the Almighty God to increase the town inhabitants, and to send down temporal blessings most plentifully among them, the people, to shew their thankfulness for the same, did resolve to build a chapel in St. Ives, they having no house in the town wherein public prayers and divine service were read, but were forced every Sunday and Holy Day to go to Lelant Church, being three miles distant from St. Ives, to hear the same; and likewise to carry their children to be baptized; their dead to be there buried; to go there to be married, and their women to be churched. Whereupon the inhabitants of St. Ives did, about the year of our Lord 1408, petition the lord Champernoun, lord of St. Ives, that he would be pleased to petition his Holiness the Pope to grant his licence for a chapel to be built within the borough. So the lord Champernoun on his petition did obtain from his Holiness the Pope Alexander the Fifth—'Primo Anno Pontificatus, Anno Domini 1410'—his Bull to build a chapel in the borough, and likewise obtained a licence from the Most Reverend Father in God the Archbishop of Canterbury, and a licence from the Reverend the Bishop of Exeter, for building the said chapel; which together with the tower was begun in the reign of King Henry the Fifth and finished in the reign of King Henry the Sixth, being sixteen years and a half in building."

The stones for building are said to have been brought by water from the neighbouring parish of Zennor. We also gather from the same source that there was a fine organ, costing £300, placed over the roodscreen, and that it was taken down by the Puritans in 1647. There is now an excellent organ at the east end of the north aisle.

A good brass of Otho Trenwith, formerly in the chancel, has been removed.

Against the wall of the chapel an epitaph, on the monument to the family of Sise, curiously commences,—

> "Neere to this bed sixe Sises late were laid,
> Foure Hopefull sonns, ye grandsire, and a maid."

According to Dr. Oliver, the patron saint is St. Ia, an Irish virgin, martyred at Hayle in Cornwall about the middle of the fifth century. Other accounts give the dedication to SS. Andrew and Peter. The standards at the east ends of two old seats—that of Master Clies and another—in the chancel, are carved with the figures of SS. Andrew and Peter. These now face the altar. Over St. Peter two kneeling figures support a shield, on which are the words, "John Peyn." The standard with the figure of St. Andrew is surmounted by two similar figures with a shield

Bench standard, St. Ives.

bearing two coats of arms impaled—1. Three pine-apples. 2. An arrow-head in pale, reversed. The arms of John Peyn, of whom Hals says, alluding to the barbarous execution of insurgents in the reign of Edward VI., "In like manner the marshal hanged John Payne, the mayor or portreeve of St. Ives, on a gallows erected in the middle of that town, whose arms are still to be seen in one of the foreseats in that church, viz. In a plain field three pine-apples."— (D. Gilbert's Hist. of Cornwall, ii. 198.) The carver had evidently never seen pine-apples. The arms are later than the carving of St. Peter beneath.

Dr. Oliver states that Pope Alexander V., Oct. 20, 1409, and John XXIII., Nov. 18, 1410, recommended Bishop Stafford to make "capellas Sancti Tewynnoci (i.e. Towednack) et Sancte Ye parochial, with font and cemetery, but dependent on Lelant."

There is a good churchyard cross recently restored.

The church of St. Ives is in excellent repair; it has been substantially reseated in oak, floor tiled, ugly galleries cleared away, and many good stained glass windows inserted. The greater part has been done by the munificence of Robert Hichens, Esq., of St. Ives and East Dulwich; who also defrayed nearly the whole of the cost for the building of the pretty church of St. John in the new parish of Halsetown, near St. Ives.

TOWEDNACK CHURCH is remarkable as alone possessing a chancel-arch among the churches of West

Cornwall; it is of the thirteenth century, very acutely pointed, and consists simply of two chamfered orders

Towednack Church.

springing from corbels, like the transept-arch at St. Gwithian [h], which is of the same date.

The church consists of chancel, nave with western tower, and south aisle and porch; the two latter are much later than the other parts.

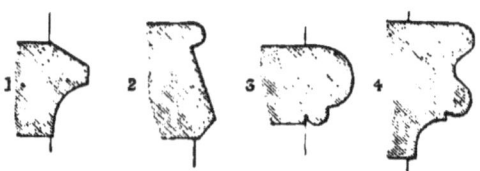

Mouldings of Tower, Towednack.
1. Cornice; 2. Battlement; 3. Stringcourse; 4. Impost, Tower-arch.

The tower, of granite, very low and massive, is altogether unlike every other in the district, and, being constructed without any attempt at orna-

[h] See above, p. 136.

mentation, proper use was made of the material at hand. The stringcourse and cornice are remarkably bold; the battlemented parapet (walled in on the east and west sides) is of the simplest character. The belfry lights are square-headed and chamfered. Altogether it is a characteristic structure, harmonizing well with its site, in the midst of a most wild and dreary region. The tower staircase, on an unusual plan, is constructed without newel or winders, and has its entrance direct from the northwest angle of the nave. The tower-arch appears to have been originally, like most others of the same date in Cornwall, a plain soffit-arch; to this responds and a chamfered order have been added. A portion of the old impost-moulding remains.

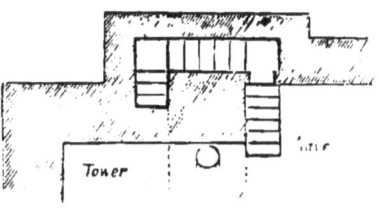

Plan of Tower Stairs, Towednack.

Incised Stone, Towednack.

The eastern bench in the porch is formed of a block of granite, 7 ft. long, 1 ft. 6 in. high, and 10 in.

wide, with an incised double cross. This stone evidently does not occupy its original position; it differs from the ordinary types of the Cornish churchyard and wayside crosses, and is most probably an early Christian sepulchral monument.

ZENNOR CHURCH, dedicated to St. Senara, stands amongst the bleak granite hills on the north coast. It has chancel, nave, western tower, north aisle, south transept, and porch. The periods of the walls may

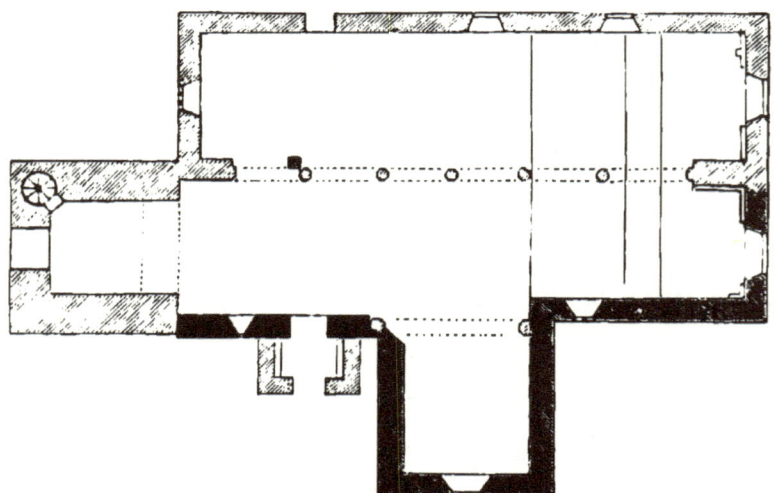

Plan of Zennor Church. Scale, 24 ft. to 1 in.

be thus briefly told,—south side of nave Norman, transept and chancel Decorated and contemporaneous: it is uncertain what the arrangement on the north side may have been when the chancel was built, but at present the nave and chancel open into an aisle by an arcade of six fifteenth-century arches, of unequal breadths, with plain octagonal granite piers. The tower, of the usual Cornish Perpendicular type, is constructed of ashlar granite, has three stages marked by plain set-offs, and a bold stringcourse above the plinth. It has a good west window, with tracery constructed of a hard black stone, nowhere to be procured in this locality, and retains the sharpness of angle and outline as freshly as when first inserted, affording a striking contrast to the disintegrated granite. Above this window occurs the rather unusual feature in this district of an ogee-headed niche, perhaps for the reception of a crucifix, which of course has long since been removed.

Norman Window, Zennor.

The nave, as at Manaccan, is wider than the chancel, and in each case the south side of the nave is older than any other part of the building. There remains westward of the doorway a single Norman light 3 ft. high by 6 in. in breadth, and with a splay of 3 ft. 3 in. through a very massive wall. This little window is of much interest as being probably the oldest to be found in the churches of West Cornwall. It is partially hidden by a gallery, concerning which the following memorandum was made in a private account-book of William Borlase, Vicar of Zennor in 1772 :—

"Memorandum, April 9th, 1794. In the year 1772, when the singing-gallery was erected, and previous to the compass-roofing of that part of the church over the gallery, I observed these figures on one of the oak sills (i.e. sills or principals) which supported the south part, 1172 or 1177, which I should take to be the date when the Church of Zenor was built, so that about the time of the Lincoln Taxation, mentioned on the other side, it was more than one hundred years old."

The doorway, also round-headed, has been so much concealed by modern repairs and repeated coats of whitewash, as to render it difficult to decide whether it is contemporaneous with the window.

The chancel is raised one step above the nave, and the sacrarium has two steps, all three extending continuously across the aisle, which has in the lower part of the east wall to the height of the window sill, masonry projecting eight inches, and a rude bracket, the upper surface of which measures 1 ft. by 1 ft. 2 in. The north wall of the aisle was rebuilt about fifty years ago.

The transept, like that at St. Levan (p. 18), probably opened into the nave by two arches ; but these, except the springing of the westernmost, with the central pillar, have been removed, and the space spanned by a wooden beam as at St. Germoe: indeed the arrangement of this church much resembles St. Germoe. The existing piers at the angles of the transept correspond to the second and fourth piers of the nave arcade; they are, in fact, of the same character and date, and take the places of others of an earlier period, or supersede some different plan of junction. There does not appear to have been a passage from the north-east angle to the chancel. The south wall is occupied by an acutely pointed window, with a plain chamfered scoinson arch, but, having lost its tracery, has been fitted with a wooden sash. The hoodmould terminations are of a type unusual in these parts.

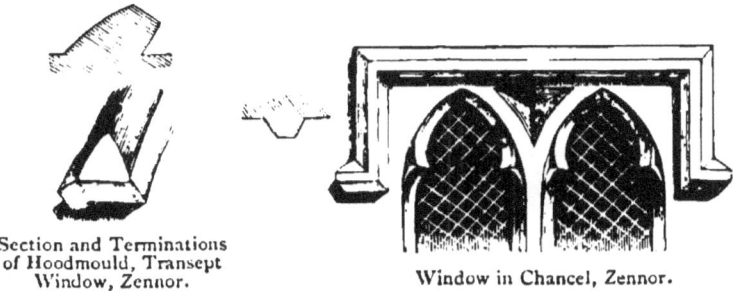

Section and Terminations of Hoodmould, Transept Window, Zennor.

Window in Chancel, Zennor.

Remains of a two-light Decorated window exist in the south wall of the chancel. It is evidently of the same date as the transept window. In all the earlier windows of this building granite was not used, but a finer grained stone procured from some distant part. The gable-cross on the transept, which was found in the chancel, and a corbel-head built into the transept wall, are of this stone. A coarse native sandstone, which I have previously noticed here and there in early work, is used in the construction of the little Norman light in the nave.

There is a good Decorated font, and two of the old bench-ends remain, one of the latter has the figure of a mermaid [1].

There are three bells, the first recast in 1717; the second and third bear the legends, SANCTE JOHANNE ORA PRO NOBIS, and SANCTA MARIA ORA PRO NOBIS.

On the edge of the cliff, near the Gurnard's Head in this parish, are the remains of an ancient chapel or oratory. Its dimensions can just be traced, and the stone altar-slab lies on the floor.

In the vicarage garden is the head of a cross of the usual Cornish type.

I have here the pleasure to thank the Rev. Wm. Borlase, Vicar of Zennor, for permission to copy from the account-book of a former Vicar the note relating to the dated sill removed from the west end of the nave, as well as for the following curious extract from the parish register:—

"Be it remembered, That on Sunday the 27th of June, 1762, Thomas Osborn of Trewey, Robert Michell of Tregarthen, Matthew Thomas of Treen, and Elizabeth Phillips of the Church Town, brought Butter and Cheese into the Chancel in the Time of Divine Service, imagining, I suppose, it would be accepted instead of their Tithes for Cows and Calves; but not being taken away either by them or any

---

[1] This bench-end and font are figured in "A Week at the Land's End."

one else before it grew offensive, I ordered the Church Wardens, under Pain of being cited to the Spiritual Court, to remove the same as an Indecency and a Nusance to the Congregation. I here insert this lest my Successor should be imposed upon by being told that I accepted of that or any other Butter and Cheese instead of Tithes of Cows and Calves, which I assure him I did not, nor of any other sort of Tithe according to the Tenor of the Terrier, dated 1727, and held in the Register of the Consistory Court of Exeter, as Witness my hand this 21st day of July, 1762, Jacob Bullock, Vicar.

"N.B. Samuel Michell, Brother of the said Robert, and [John] Baragwanath were Church Wardens, [and removed] the said Butter and Cheese as a [Nusance at] my command.—J. B., V^r."

The words between brackets are now almost illegible in the register.

The Church of ST. HILARY, with the exception of the tower and spire, was destroyed by fire on the night of Good Friday, 1853. At that time it consisted of chancel, nave, and north and south aisles, all, excepting perhaps the chancel, later than the tower. When the church was rebuilt some few alterations were found necessary to be made in the tower, but it retains its original principal features, and differs altogether from every other tower of the district. It is of early Decorated date, and from the near connexion of St. Hilary Church with St. Michael's Mount, builders of a better class than usual may have had to do with its construction.

Buttresses extend nearly half the height of the tower; they have bold set-offs, chamfered angles, and cappings. The angles of the tower have round mouldings, and there are corbels along the cornice. The belfry windows are of three lights. Each alternate spire-light is blocked, the space being occupied by sculptured heads and other ornaments. The tower-arch is recessed and chamfered, and has three-quarter-round responds with moulded capitals and bases.

Blocked Spire-light, St. Hilary.

During the rebuilding of the church fragments of early work were found, and a portion of the capital of a pier now in the churchyard shews mouldings and ornamentation unlike any existing work in West Cornwall churches.

Through the exertions of the Vicar, the Rev. Thomas Pascoe, who contributed largely to the fund, a handsome church has been built on to the old tower.

Tower, St. Hilary.

ST. SITHNEY CHURCH has shallow transepts added to the north and south aisles. The Perpendicular tower is superior to many others of the same period, and has a boldly moulded tower-arch, and shafted pinnacles, with figures of the Evangelists at their bases, resting on the cornice.

The east window of the north aisle, like that at St. Cury, is of four lights with geometrical tracery, and has the splay of the arch internally filled with geometrical ornamentation in panels.

On the chancel floor is a portion of a brass cross: the word "Mercy" was inscribed on each limb, and beneath the following words may still be read:— "Hic jacet Rogerus Trelbythyanyk cujus anime propicietur Deus. Amen." On the wall of the south aisle is a neat brass, date 1856, in memory of the Rev. John Rogers, M.A., of Penrose, Canon of Exeter.

ST. CROWAN CHURCH possesses no features of particular interest. It has a fine tower with a peal of six bells, and a square Norman font with dragons at the base; being found in a mutilated condition it was repaired, and the shaft is modern.

The numerous monuments and brasses of the ancient family of St. Aubyn in this church are figured in Polwhele's "History of Cornwall."

CAMBORNE CHURCH, dedicated to St. Meriadoc, has recently been re-seated and otherwise restored. Many of the original Perpendicular windows remain. The piers and capitals are of the usual type, and the tower resembles others already noticed. The panels of the pulpit are carved with the symbols of the Passion: one shield bears the five wounds, representing the wells of pity, comfort, grace, mercy and everlasting life; from the heart (the well of everlasting life) blood flows into a chalice.

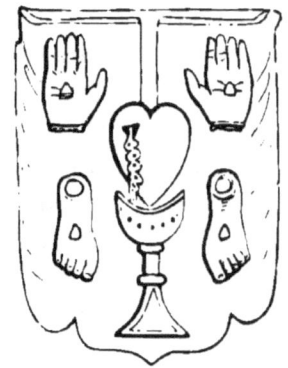

Symbols of the Five Wounds, Camborne.

Against the exterior of the wall of the porch is a very ancient altar-slab. It is figured in Borlase's "Antiquities of Cornwall," and bears the following inscription:—"Leuiut jusit hec Altare pro anima sua."

The walls of the sanctuary are of the fourteenth century; a good piscina and a fine old stoup were discovered during the late restoration.

NOTE.—Since these papers were printed, a restoration of St. Just Church has been commenced; and, as is generally the case, some interesting discoveries have been made. On the authority of Mr. Buller, ("Account of the Parish of St. Just-in-Penwith," p. 19,) it was stated that the whole of the old sanctuary walls were removed when the east end of the church was rebuilt in 1834, and this appeared to be the case. But the stripping of the plaster proves that the lower part of the south wall was retained, including the piscina and a single sedile, somewhat resembling those in the neighbouring church of St. Madron, and evidently portions of the church which was consecrated in 1336 by Bishop Grandisson.

Some mural paintings have also been discovered on the north wall of the north aisle. The designs are bordered by the running pattern of rude foliage twisted round a straight continuous stem, so common on capitals and woodwork of the fifteenth century. There can still be traced a representation of St. George and the Dragon; also a large figure surrounded by a curious collection of quaint devices—scales, an anvil and hammer, a horn, part of a mermaid, the tail and comb remaining, a rake, a ladder, a boat bearing a fish, &c.

Beneath this painting the workmen found that some of the wall had been removed, and a rough recess formed, 2 ft. 7 in. by 1 ft. 2 in., and 2 ft. deep. It contained a skull and other human bones (possibly relics secreted at the Reformation), and some pieces of stained glass, which appear to have been hastily deposited, and then walled up.

The present, with the preceding papers, may serve to give some idea of the ecclesiology of western Cornwall. As, however, each church has been referred to separately, and its details described with but incidental comparison with others, it will be desirable to offer a few general remarks on the whole.

MATERIAL. The Perpendicular work of Cornwall differs in many respects from that of other parts of the kingdom, chiefly, as might be expected, from local causes, of which perhaps the most influential was material. Granite, deliberately rejected by mediæval builders in favour of stones capable of higher finish, came into use in the fifteenth and sixteenth centuries, and where it was plentiful, hurried on debasement. Indeed, granite is totally unfit for delicate workmanship, even if, at the time, it be well worked, being frequently thickly studded with pieces of felspar, which coming on sharp angles, get thrown out by exposure to the atmosphere, and the sharpness of outline soon becomes effaced. It may be seen on most of the exposed granite towers how the angles have fretted away, and such sculpture as was attempted has been reduced to almost shapeless masses.

The granite then used was commonly called "moorstone," i.e. blocks found lying above the surface on the open moor. These, being ready at hand, were carted away without much attempt at selection. It was wretchedly inferior to the granite now procured from deep and extensive working in quarries; the finer or coarser qualities being applied to the purposes for which they are best adapted. Still, granite should only be employed in large bold masses; and where the old builders judiciously confined themselves to plain mouldings, as in Towednack tower, and produced variety and change of line by simple chamferings, the effect is in most instances pleasing and characteristic.

The fine towers of St. Probus and St. Austell, in East Cornwall, shew great skill in the use of granite, and the granite tower at St. Ives would be a very fine structure if the buttresses were not so lean and poor.

In the earliest work Caen and other free-stones were much used, and even in the latest Perpendicular churches a finer-grained stone was occasionally procured for window tracery and for the mouldings of the principal doorways.

GROUND-PLANS. To the casual observer the greater number of the Cornish churches seem to be fashioned after one model, and to belong to one style—the Perpendicular. The reconstruction or rebuilding of the earlier fabrics which took place in the fifteenth century more or less throughout the country, appears to have been carried to an unusual extent in the far west. Whatever may have been the cause elsewhere, it is very clear that in Cornwall, at all events, increased population had little or nothing to do with the increased zeal in church building. The country districts were but thinly inhabited —a few miners' cottages scattered over the wild downs and moors, little groups of fishermen's huts here and there along the coast; towns small and unimportant, and having no extensive trade or manufactures, were not calculated to attract settlers from distant parts. Although there were some families of distinction, the people generally were not rich. Yet with all these drawbacks we find many of the churches, even in the most remote places, of unusually large dimensions, much larger in proportion than the ordinary parish churches of the rich midland counties, and of more populous districts. That the churches are nearly all alike in respect of their plans is to some extent true, and there is but little diversity of outline.

The earliest examples of ecclesiastical building in Cornwall are perhaps to be found amongst the little chapels and oratories, such as St. Piran's, St. Gothian's, St. Madron's Baptistery, &c. Because these do not possess any external sign of distinction between chancel and nave, it has been supposed that they afforded the type for the non-chancel-arched churches of the fifteenth and sixteenth centuries. It is rare now to find in this district[k] a chancel-arch; but we have sufficient proof that some did exist, and were destroyed when, in the fifteenth and sixteenth centuries, the transepts of the Early English and Decorated churches were removed for long aisles.

[k] And in the county generally: the fine churches of St. Michael Penkivel and Shevioke have come down to us nearly unaltered; both have arches to the transepts, but a continuous unbroken roof to chancel and nave; both are of the fourteenth century.

It would appear, therefore, that the ancient oratories had little or no influence on the mediæval builders. Internally, however, these ancient structures have some distinguishing mark separating chancel and nave, such as a step, or a raised altar platform, and at St. Gothian's oratory[1] a shallow projecting wall of masonry on either side.

There is scarcely a parish in Cornwall in which there are not the ruins of some ancient chapel or oratory, and where such remains do not exist tradition generally points out the sites on which they formerly stood. Many estates have a "chapel field," or in the Cornish, *parc-an-chapel*. In several instances where the buildings have been removed, crosses mark the spots. Most of these chapels bear the names of saints whose names are not connected with the parish churches, and of whose history nothing is known. These pious wanderers seem to have erected little cells in lonely spots, by the side of some spring or well, and thus a peculiar sanctity became attached to those places, of which the remembrance has not yet altogether died out. It was in the earlier days of British Christianity when these Irish missionaries gave their names to such localities, and of course we look in vain for the little structures they first erected. Whether of stone or wood may perhaps have depended on which material was at hand; at any rate, these crumbled away in the course of time. But to keep alive the memories of these saints, pious men

---

[1] See above, p. 139.

in later days, from time to time, re-erected the walls on the original plans, and continued to use the buildings as chapels, oratories, and baptisteries. Much of this work was done in the fifteenth century, and many of these detached buildings appear to have answered the purpose for which chantries were in some places added to the parish churches. Indeed, it will be found that the greater number of the Cornish chapels as they now exist, date no further back than the fifteenth century, and many of the crosses are not more ancient. The oratory of St. Piran-in-the-Sands may be as early as Saxon times, and the oratory of St. Gothian is in all probability as old. Few others, however, have such claims to antiquity. The examples referred to may be considered as amongst the earliest Christian structures in Cornwall, and are valuable as witnesses to the ritual arrangement of the age in which they were built.

The absence of mouldings has in many cases rendered it difficult to assign a date to these chapels; they are so uniform in plan and so rudely built, that at a hasty glance some might be referred to the twelfth or thirteenth century, until the fortunate discovery of a window-head or door-jamb in a kindred building affords a clue to their age. The style of the masonry is not always a certain guide in this district, for modern walls of the cottages of the poor, if found in ruins, with no doorways or windows, might almost be classed with what is called Cyclopean masonry. The walls of cottages and outhouses are often formed of great shapeless blocks, sometimes reaching nearly up to the roof, the intervening spaces being filled with rubble. Nothing can have a ruder or more primitive appearance. Indeed, it is the style of the first builders in these parts, of the men who raised the hill forts and the hut circles. In this we see the effect of material on architecture: buildings must in a greater or less degree, of course, partake of the natural characteristics of the country, especially when but little labour or money is to be had. The humble Cornish builder of ancient and modern times set in huge masses of granite just as he found them, and the larger they were the better they answered his purpose; if he could make three or four great blocks of stone form a wall, the less labour and skill was required in building, and the main object was attained. And as both old and modern walls are found constructed without the use of cement—nothing more than dry stone walling—and as this mode seems to have been continued from the earliest to the latest times, it would in many instances, apart from other aid, increase the difficulty of assigning a date, and lead many unacquainted with these local characteristics into error.

Some of the first churches occupying the sites of these stations of holy men, may have consisted merely of chancel and nave, but many of early date were cruciform in plan; of this fact proofs have been given in noticing the Early English work at Manaccan.

Cornish Churches. 167

When a transept exists, it is in most instances contemporaneous with the chancel. The occurrence of one transept only—either on the north or south—has been considered a great puzzle, and a peculiarity in Cornish churches. A correspondent of the GENTLEMAN'S MAGAZINE in 1781, asks for an explanation:—

"In almost all the Cornish churches," he writes, "(at least those I have seen,) there is a singularity which I have not observed in churches elsewhere. . . . I cannot conceive for what purpose this half-transept, if I may give it such a name, was added to the church when the building was erected, as it is now seldom used for seats for any part of the congregation."

By careful examination it may be found that these "half-transepts" are truly half-transepts, and that the missing half has been merged into a north (or south) aisle, as in the accompanying diagram. This

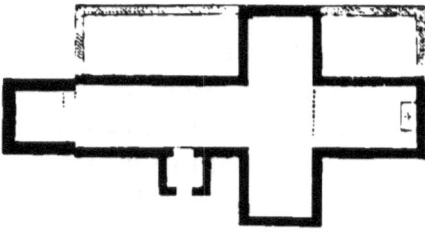

Plan of Church.

shews how many churches were treated in the fifteenth century. The north transept, with the exception of its north wall, and the north walls of the chancel and nave, were removed, and an arcade substituted. Thus we have a church of chancel, nave with western tower, north or south transept, as the case may be, and north or south aisle. Examples of both will be found in the preceding pages. The manner in which the transept and nave are connected is sometimes by a single arch, sometimes by two arches, like the beginning of an arcade; as if it had been the intention to supersede the transept for an aisle, and the idea afterwards abandoned. The double-arched transepts may, however, be an original constructional feature. At Zennor, St. Germoe, and St. Mawgan, the arches are removed, and the space spanned by a wooden beam. Some churches have shallow transepts to the aisles, but these are always the latest additions to the building, and appear to have been constructed for the special use of the principal families in the neighbourhood, as at St. Mawgan, St. Breage, and St. Germoe.

Many churches of the fifteenth century were undoubtedly from their commencement designedly continuous, but in those when it was possible the sanctuary of the original church was preserved, but arch after arch was added westward opening into aisles, extending along both nave and chancel. These continuous aisles are generally somewhat narrower than the nave, but are of the same height; and the long unbroken roofs in three parallel ridges, sometimes in four where a side chapel is added, as at St. Ives and St. Gwinear (see next page), have a very monotonous and tame effect. In some instances the eastern walls of the aisles are flush with that of the chancel; in others the chancel projects by the sanctuary, as at St. Madron.

St. Gwinear Church.

THE ROODSCREENS were the grand features of demarcation between chancel and nave, and in the two-aisled churches were carried across the whole building, with a roodloft-staircase in the wall of the north or south aisle. At St. Madron, the screen ran, not from pier to pier, but clear of all the piers, under the apices of the arches; the furthest departure possible from the chancel-arch plan.

TOWERS. The towers are in almost every instance placed at the west end of the nave. The greater number are of three stages, some are of four, each receding a little to the parapet, which is brought out to the plane of the base. In the Land's End district they are built of ashlar blocks of granite, with but little attempt at ornamentation. At St. Germoe, St. Ludgvan, and St. Gwithian, however, the pinnacles are richly panelled and sculptured with quatrefoils; gargoyles are placed under the cornice, and, as in other towers not so highly ornamented, the pinnacles rest on angels. The granite tower pinnacles present some originality of design characteristic of the material employed. The pinnacle of Sancreed tower is an example of the effect obtained by the simple process of chamfering. The shaft rising from the parapet is chamfered at each angle; above is a plain moulding, embattled, to receive the octagonal pinnacle, which is finished with a chamfered block and cable-moulding; the whole surmounted by a ball. At St. Just the pinnacles are square shafts with plain round and hollow mouldings, and a sort of scallop pattern as a substitute for battlements, from which the capping rises square, and surmounted by a ball and cross. In octagonal-shafted pinnacles this scalloping becomes more fully developed, and has a corona-like appearance. The shafts are sometimes

Pinnacle, Sancreed.

Pinnacle, St. Just.

panelled and battlemented, and the pinnacle finished with ball and cross. The pinnacle of the staircase-turret at Gwinear terminates with a triple moulding. The pinnacles of St. Perran-uthnoe, of a very plain character, finish with a cross placed horizontally, which arrangement occurs again in the churches of the Lizard district.

The parapets are battlemented.

The staircase is either in the thickness of the north wall, or is contained in a square or octagonal turret.

Many of the tower-arches are simply plain soffit arches, others have good and bold mouldings.

These notes apply chiefly to the Perpendicular towers; indeed, with the exception of two or three, they are all of that style.

St. Mawgan, perhaps the best tower in west Cornwall (see p. 172), and somewhat earlier than the rest (excepting St. Hilary), has fine pinnacles of clustered shafts (see p. 173).

The characteristic features of the towers of the Lizard district have been already described in the notice of the church of St. Ruan Major[m].

The granite towers are to be noted for their plainness, which, however, harmonizes well with much of the wild and exposed country in which they are situated. Many stand on high ground, and doubtless served as landmarks. Indeed it is attested that a yearly allowance was made by the port of St. Ives for the white-washing of St. Hilary tower, so as to

[m] See above, p. 94.

render it more conspicuous at sea. St. Burian tower is the first building seen by mariners approaching England from the westward, and it is remarkable that three of the loftiest towers in West Cornwall,

Church of St. Mawgan in Meneage.

St. Paul, St. Gwinear, and St. Burian, are all built on high land, and in each the staircase-turret is carried considerably above the parapet, resembling the watch-towers which occur in some districts, and of which the tower of Llandrillo yn Rhos on the north coast of Wales affords an example. It has also been suggested that these turrets were used as beacons. Numerous instances of lanterns constructed on towers might be given, but that it was the custom in this part of the kingdom it may be sufficient to refer to the lantern — more popularly known as St. Michael's Chair—on the tower of St. Michael's Mount, which was undoubtedly designed for this purpose.

Turret, St. Burian.

Some of the ordinary types of the towers are figured in the preceding pages. A cut of St. Ruan Minor (see p. 174) is annexed as an interesting specimen of late fifteenth or early sixteenth-century work, pleasing because so unambitious. It is not, however, entirely of granite.

Of the churches described in these papers two only have towers with spires, namely, St. Keverne, a Perpendicular building, and St. Hilary, a good example of early fourteenth-century architecture. Indeed, spires are nearly as rare in Cornwall as chancel arches.

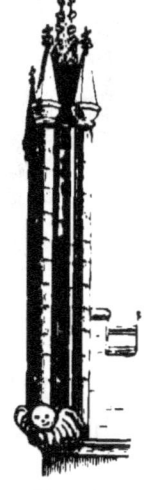

Pinnacle, St. Mawgan.

WINDOWS.—For many of the best windows, as I have elsewhere noted, a finer-grained stone was procured, even for those of Perpendicular date. Most of the later windows are, however, of granite, and

Church of St. Ruan Minor.

this doubtless accounts in great measure for their meagre and poor appearance, though there are interesting examples of its adaptation to this purpose with the best results. In the latter part of the fifteenth and beginning of the sixteenth century, windows of two, three, or four pointed lights, with sunk spandrels, within a square head, were frequently inserted. Another common design is that of three or four lights under a depressed four-centred arch. If of three lights, the centre one is carried up to the head, that on each side terminating at the springing of the enclosing arch, the spaces over them being pierced. When there are four, the two middle lights are carried up to the head, (fig. 1); but in some cases the lights follow the form of the head of the window with spandrels sunk, (fig. 2). A very frequent form is shewn by the annexed figure, (fig. 3). It has a

Fig. 1.   Fig. 2.   Fig. 3.

Decorated character, but occurs in the latest work, probably in imitation of the earlier forms. The spaces between the lights and the enclosing arch

Window and Cusp, Gunwalloe.

are in some cases pierced, in others left blank. In the larger windows of this kind the upper openings are formed by the tracery being carried up in a reticulated pattern from the heads of the lights beneath, as at St. Ruan and St. Ives. Gunwalloe Church affords an example of a late window of two lights with a quatrefoil in the head, the cusps of the quatrefoil terminating in flowers. This peculiar cusping occurs in other churches of the Lizard district. A two-light, square-headed window at St. Antony has cusps of this kind, and the sinking in the spandrel contains a ball. This treatment of spandrels may be seen also at St. Mawgan and elsewhere.

Window, St. Mawgan.

Window, St. Erth.

Many windows of the fifteenth century have geometrical tracery, evidently copies by less skilful hands of earlier work. The annexed examples from St. Erth and St. Antony may be transitional from De-

Window, St. Just.

Window, St. Antony.

corated to Perpendicular. There are a few examples of a tendency to the Flamboyant, and at St. Just is a rare instance, perhaps unique in this district, of a window with divergent tracery.

THE ROOFS are all of the barrel or waggon form, with braces and purlins, sometimes plainly moulded, sometimes richly carved, and large bosses at the intersections. The blank spaces between are plastered, except at St. Ives, where the squares are boarded and enriched with surface ornamentation over the sanctuary. A continuous pattern is frequently carved on the wall-plate, and in some churches—St. Ives, St. Madron, and St. Mawgan—full-length figures of angels, standing on corbels, symbolically representing the heavenly host, are placed at the springings of the braces. Originally the woodwork was richly painted and gilded, as may still be seen at St. Levan.

PORCHES.—There is a type of porch found at St. Burian, St. Just, St. Breage, and St. Wendron which owes its peculiarity to the use of granite. The St. Burian porch may be taken as the best example of the group. It is a large structure, built of ashlar, buttressed where it joins the wall of the aisle, and doubly buttressed at the outer angles. Commencing at the base, there is a bold plinth, then a stringcourse carried round the buttresses; above this the buttresses have a plain set-off, and finish with a characteristic capping—cubes with their angles bevelled—thus presenting five triangular surfaces. From this rises a pinnacle, panelled and crocketed. These crockets, too, are peculiar; there is no attempt at the real crocket, a budding or unfolding leaf—moorstone would not admit of this—but they are merely "billets," if they may be so called, not of themselves elegant, but producing a certain effect, and witnessing to the good sense of the designer. The graceful flowing line to be produced in free-stone could not be rendered, so the workman stopped when he could

Porch, St. Burian.

safely go no further. Attempts at curved crockets result in a flame-like figure, as at St. Mullion and Ludgvan, the "billets" being sharpened away at the top.

The parapet of the porch projects from the wall, and has battlements of bold and effective construction. The doorway is a depressed four-centred arch, under a square head, with plain wide mouldings and spandrels filled with quatrefoils.

Pinnacle, St. Mullion.

MOULDINGS AND SCULPTURE.—The difficulties experienced in dealing with the native material may also be observed in the mouldings of the piers. Many are plain octangular pillars, and many consist of four half, or three-quarter round shafts, with intervening cavetto or ogee mouldings. Sometimes these shafts are attached to a square centre pier, of which the points of the angles just peep out between, as at St. Perran-uthnoe and St. Sennen. The section of one of the Sancreed piers shews circular central pillar, to which four three-quarter round shafts are attached.

Section of Pier, Sancreed.

The bases and capitals are also peculiar. The better kind of capitals, and these are numerous, are those of the bell form, with angular mouldings: examples occur at St. Perran-uthnoe and St. Burian. Where ornament and foliage are attempted, the result, as might be expected, is generally far from satisfactory, though occasionally when the design is simple the effect is good. A cross within a lozenge, for instance, which occurs at St. Breage[n], and in other churches, is much more successfully rendered in granite than flowing foliage. This last is found in many of the granite churches, and the leaves in almost every instance are either cramped and formal or most graceless and commonplace. Another favourite ornament was a series of expanded flowers, and two connected leaves within branches arranged like the zigzag moulding are very common[n].

Flower Ornament.

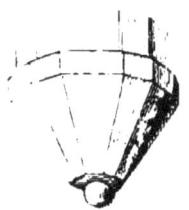

Impost, St. Levan.

The door-jambs and arches have mouldings of two or three orders, and the plinth-mouldings of some of the towers are very bold and effective. The imposts of the tower-arches are also often characteristic. Those at St. Levan, St. Sennen, and Sancreed may serve as examples. The latter has the section of a Norman impost, and it is worthy of note that some of the ornamentation of the fifteenth-century churches has the appearance of being copied from Norman work. The frequent occurrence of the cable-moulding may be especially referred to. One instance has been given in the Sancreed pinnacle, and a late capital at Gunwalloe may serve as another.

[n] See above, p. 113.

Some of the fifteenth-century fonts also appear to be copies of those of a much earlier period.

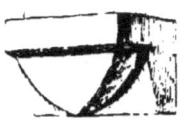 

Impost, St. Sennen.   Impost, Sancreed.

A few of the gable crosses are pleasing examples of what may be done by mere chamfering. The annexed cut represents that on the porch of St. Ruan

Capital, Gunwalloe.   Cross, St. Ruan Major.   Stoup, Sancreed.

Major. There is at Sancreed a good stoup similarly treated.

The existing Perpendicular and debased buildings are not the true Cornish church. In some parts of the county, however, good examples of the latter still remain, such as St. Antony in Roseland, St. Michael Penkivel, St. Ive, Shevioke, and Southill; to which architects would do well to refer when about to erect or restore churches in Cornwall.

It is proposed to give, at some future time, a few notes on, and illustrations of, some of the churches of East Cornwall, possessing much good Norman and Early English work.

Though many of the Cornish churches are still in a very dilapidated condition, and sadly need restoration, it is gratifying to know that much has been done in this way of late years, and that several new churches have been erected in populous districts.

NAMES OF THE PATRON SAINTS OF THE CHURCHES DESCRIBED IN THIS VOLUME.

(From Dr. Oliver's *Monasticon Diœcesis Exoniensis*.)

Parish, whether Rectory, Vicarage, or Perpetual Curacy.	Deanery.	Date of Dedication and Saint.	Remarks.
Anthony, St., *V.*, in Meneage, often called Antoninus the Martyr	Kerrier	St. Anthony	Dependent on Tywardreth Priory.
Breage, *V.*, with Germoe, Gunwalloe, and Cury	Kerrier	St. Breaca	
Burian, St., *R.*, with St. Levan and St. Sennen *	Penwith	Aug. 26, 1238, St. Buriana	Festival kept May 29. In the *Inquisitiones Nonarum*, p. 348, "capella Sancti Silvani" is mentioned.
Camborne, *R.*	Penwith	St. Meriadocus	Sometimes called, in later times, St. Martin, in the registers.
Crowan, *V.*	Penwith	St. Crewena	Bronescombe's Register, fol. 41 : a chapel here was dedicated to St. Augustine.
Cury, *olim* St. Corentine, *V.*, with Breage, Gunwalloe, and Germoe	Kerrier	St. Corentinus	What is now Cury parish was formerly within the parish of St. Corentinus, and contained a small chapel, licensed by Bishop Stafford in favour of the monks of Hales, who might come down to visit their property there.
Erth, St., *V.*	Penwith	St. Ercus	There was a saint of this name, the first bishop of Slane, anno 513. Can St. Ercus be a corruption of St. Enurchus, the bishop of Orleans 340,

* On the death of Dean Stanhope, April, 1864, the parishes of St. Burian, St. Levan, and St. Sennen, were constituted into three separate Rectories, which are in the patronage of the Prince of Wales.

Names of the Patron Saints, &c.

Parish, whether Rectory, Vicarage, or Perpetual Curacy.	Deanery.	Date of Dedication and Saint.	Remarks.
			whose feast in the calendar is marked September 7? St. Mary Magdalene's Chapel at Boswythgy, licensed July 20, 1398.
Felack, St., or Phillack, *R.*, and Gwithian	Penwith	St. Felicitas	Virgin Martyr. Bishop Bronescombe assigned to the vicar of St. Felicitas all the obventions of its church and of Connerton Chapel (the tithe of its sheaf excepted), as also a glebe of five acres, with the tithes of sheaf de Runnier, Penpol, Nanteren, and Trethinegy (Reg., fol. 7).
Gulval, or Lanesly, *V.*	Penwith	St. Gudwal	St. Gudwal, a British saint, flourished in the sixth century in this diocese, whose feast was kept June 6. An ancient calendar styles him bishop of St. Malo.
Gunwalloe, *V.*, with Breage, Germoe, and Cury	Kerrier	St. Winwolaus	Of noble Welsh extraction; Abbot of Landevenack in Bretagne, ob. March 3, 529.
Gwinear, *V.*	Penwith	St. Winnierus	
Gwithian and Fillack, *R.*	Penwith	St. Gothianus	
Hilary, St., or Ilarii, *V.*, with Hermes, chapel of		St. Hilary	On March 22, 1309, Bishop Stapeldon allowed the inhabitants of Marazion to have service three times a-week in St. Hermes Chapel there (Reg., fol. 39). The chapel was rebuilt and reopened Sept. 9, 1839.
Ives, St., *C.*	Penwith	St. Ilya, Ia, or Ya	St. Ifia, an Irish virgin, said to have died at Hayle, in Cornwall, about the middle of the fifth century. Pope Alexander V. (Oct. 28, 1409) and John XXIII. (Nov. 18, 1410) recommended Bishop Stafford to make "capellas Sancti Tewynnoci et Sancte

Names of the Patron Saints, &c.

Parish, whether Rectory, Vicarage, or Perpetual Curacy.	Deanery.	Date of Dedication and Saint.	Remarks.
			Ye" parochial, with font and cemetery, but dependent on Lelant.
Just, St., *V.*	Penwith	St. Justus	
Keverne, St., *V.*	Kerrier	St. Keveran, or Kieran	Bishop Nevil's Reg., fol. 21; appropriated to the Abbey of Beaulient, Dec. 5, 1330.
Landewednack, *R.*	Kerrier	St. Winwolaus	The chapel of the Holy Cross at Rosewyk was dedicated by Bishop Broncscombe on Easter Day, 1261.
Lelant Uny, *olim* Lanant with St. Towednack, *V.*	Penwith	St. Ewinus	The papal recommendation to Bishop Stafford to erect St. Tewynnoc into a parochial chapel was not carried into effect, as St. Ives was, till a hundred and thirty years later, viz. June 27, 1542, when Bishop Vesey directed his suffragan, William of Hippo, to consecrate his cemetery.
Levan, St., *R.*, with St. Burian and St. Sennen	Penwith	St. Livinus	Perhaps St. Livin, the Irish bishop who preached the Christian faith in Belgium, and is said to have been martyred at Escha, near Hanthen, in the district of Alost, Nov. 12, A.D. 656. His feast-day is kept in the parish on Oct. 15, perhaps the day of the translation of his relics. —*Monasticon*, p. 8.
Ludgvan, or Ludevon, *R.*	Penwith	St. Ludowanus	
Madron, or Madern, *V.*, with Morva	Penwith	St. Madernus, or Paternus	Chapel of St. Morwetha licensed April 17, 1409; of St. Bridget, Oct. 28, 1437; of St. Mary, Penzance, June 15, 1397; and of St. Gabriel and St. Raphael, at Penzance, Aug. 12, 1429.
Manacon, or Manathon, *V.*	Kerrier	St. Antoninus	

Parish, whether Rectory, Vicarage, or Perpetual Curacy.	Deanery.	Date of Dedication and Saint.	Remarks.
Mawgan, St., and Martin, St., *R*.	Kerrier	St. Mawganus	
Mullion, *V*.	Kerrier	St. Melanus	This abbot in Brittany, born in South Wales, was the friend of St. Sampson, and died about 617. He is often called St. Meen.
Paul, St., *V*.	Penwith	St. Paulinus	Chapel of St. Mary, at Mousehole, often occurs in the registers.
Perran - Uthnoe, *R*., (Lanuthnoe, Bronescombe's Reg. fol. 41)	Penwith	St. Pieran	St. James' Chapel, at Goldsithney, licensed July 12, 1450.
Ruan-Major, *R*.	Kerrier	St. Rumonus	
Ruan-Minor, *R*.	Kerrier	St. Rumonus	Often described as "in terrâ aridâ."
Sancreed, St., *V*.	Penwith	St. Sancredus	
Sennen, St., *R*., with St. Burian and St. Levan	Penwith	St. Senan	St. Sennen, or Senan, an Irish bishop and bosom friend of St. David of Wales, ob. March 1, about 544. Some say he accompanied St. Burian into Cornwall; his feast was on the Sunday nearest to St. Andrew's.—*Monasticon*, p. 9.
Sithney, *V*.	Kerrier	St. Siduinus, or Sithuinus	Query, St. Swithun?
Towednack, *V*., with Uny Lelant	Penwith		
Wendron, St., with Helston, *V*.	Kerrier	St. Wendrona	A chapel at Merther Park, in the parish of St. Wendron, dedicated to St. Decumanus, licensed Aug. 18, 1427.
Zennor, or Senar, *V*.	Penwith	St. Senara	

TWO DAYS IN CORNWALL WITH THE CAMBRIAN ARCHÆOLOGICAL ASSOCIATION.

In compliance with an invitation from the Royal Institution of Cornwall, the meeting of the Cambrian Archæological Association in 1862 was held at Truro, whence excursions were made to different parts of the county.

The members arrived at Truro on Monday, August 25th, and the two following days were devoted to the neighbourhoods of Bodmin and Truro. On Thursday a large party left for Penzance. Every facility was kindly offered by the directors of the West Cornwall Railway. The weather could not possibly have been finer; and it is only to be regretted that more time was not available for the examination of the numerous antiquities scattered within a radius of five or six miles around the town.

A few of the members proceeded by the first morning train to the Marazion station, visiting St. Michael's Mount, and the inscribed stones at St. Hilary. The greater number, however, came on by the next train, joining the others at Penzance, where carriages were waiting to drive westward.

Trembath Cross.

After leaving the outskirts of the town, the first object noticed by the wayside was the ancient cross at Trembath.

It is of the usual form of the Cornish cross, a plain shaft with a rounded head, but differs from any other in the county in the rude figures incised on two of its sides. On the eastern face is a patriarchal cross. Possibly it may have marked the boundary of land of, or have been in some other way connected with, a religious Order holding land in the neighbourhood. The canons regular of the Order of the Holy Sepulchre, for instance, bore on the cassock a cross of similar form.

At Drift, about a mile beyond this cross, we passed the two pillars described and figured by Borlase ("Antiquities of Cornwall," p. 187), and soon after the tall Tregonebris stone was seen. We did not, however, alight from the carriages to inspect those objects, as better examples of monuments of this class were to be visited in the course of the day. We had now advanced about six miles on the

Boscawen-ûn Circle.

Land's End road, and were opposite the Boscawen-ûn Circle, which lay in a moor on the left, a quarter of a mile distant. Nearly all the party went to inspect this remarkable circle, which is formed by nineteen stones, averaging little more than three feet in height, and placed at irregular distances, some being thirteen feet apart, others no more than seven or eight. Within the area, but not in the centre, is a stone nine feet long, in an inclining position. It inclines W.S.W. 49° from the horizon, but whether originally upright is uncertain. No other stone circle in Cornwall has this peculiarity, which is found, however, in the tall stones in the "ship-barrows" of Sweden, and marks probably the site of some structural arrangement.

The diameter from east to west is seventy-six feet, from north to south eighty-one feet. Dr. Borlase speaks of a cromlech on the north-eastern side. This does not now exist; but a large stone lies near the spot, and may have formed a side or covering for a kist-vaen.

It is unnecessary here to give the numerous speculations as to the use of this Circle, but it may not be out of place to say that the late Rev. Thomas Price considered this to be the Circle mentioned in an ancient Welsh triad, whatever importance may be attached to it, as "the Gorsedd of Boscawen in Damnonium."

About thirty yards south-east of the Circle is a barrow from six to seven feet high.

At the time of our visit the Boscawen-ûn Circle was divided by a hedge, and many of the stones were overgrown by brambles and furze. Recently, however, these disfigurements and obstructions have been cleared away. The Circle has been enclosed within a strong fence, and is now secure from accidental or wilful mutilation. For this care taken of a valuable monument of a remote age, the county owes a debt of gratitude to Miss Elizabeth Carne, of Penzance, on whose property the Circle stands, and who has thus set an excellent example to Cornish landholders to preserve those antiquities for which the county is so justly celebrated, but which are in too many instances liable to destruction by thoughtless and ignorant tenants [a].

[a] In anticipation of a visit, in the autumn of 1864, from the members of the Royal Institution of Cornwall and of the Penzance Natural History and Antiquarian Society, trenches had been cut within the Circle, but nothing of interest appears to have been discovered. The large barrow mentioned above, on being dug into, was considered by those who conducted the operations to have been previously opened. There was found, however, on its north side the remains of a kist-vaen, and nearer its centre, in a line, three circular pits, each about one foot in diameter, and covered with flat stones. Two only contained ashes.

A barrow sixty yards south-west from the Circle, on being examined, also shewed signs of being previously opened.

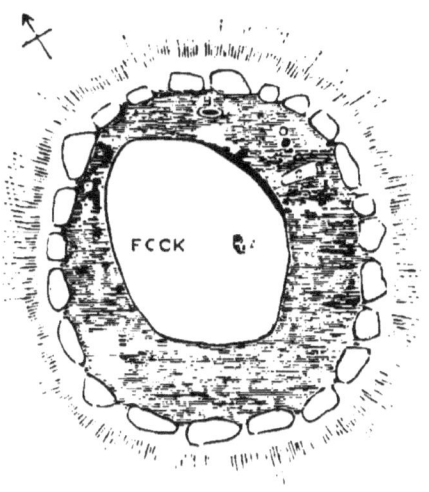

Plan of Barrow, near Boscawen-ûn Circle.

Its construction is remarkable, consisting of a circle of stones set around a large granite rock, twelve feet by eleven feet, and two feet ten inches thick, with a smooth upper surface in which is sunk a cavity, A, one foot six inches in length by one foot one inch as its greatest breadth. This upper part of the rock appears originally to have been exposed to view, though it had become overgrown by vegetation, and formed the summit of the barrow. Between the enclosing circle and the rock is a space with an average breadth of four feet, in which were found, at B, at the depth of eighteen inches, a piece of

Cornish Antiquities.

After a pleasant scramble through heath and gorse, we regained the carriages on the high road, and proceeded

granite, eighteen inches in length by twelve inches in breadth, and about nine inches thick, scooped out on one side to the depth of four inches. It is but the fragment of some instrument, for evidently the

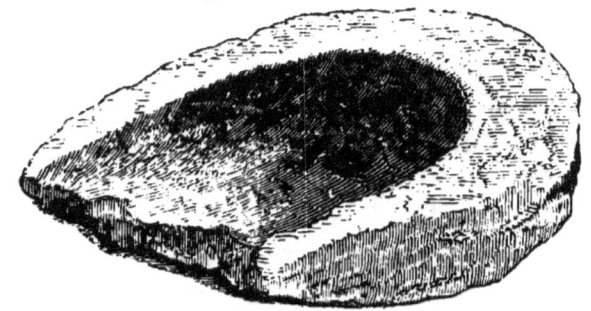

Stone found in a Barrow, near the Boscawen-ûn Circle.

stone has been broken across. The surface of the hollowed part appears to have been subjected to friction, as if a muller had been worked in it for the purpose of bruising or grinding grain *. At C, a stone two feet six inches long and about the same breadth, set on its edge, and rising nearly to the surface of the barrow; on its south side were a number of small loose stones; on the north side many calcined human bones, fragments of large urns, and a small one entire, mouth downwards, filled with soil. It measures in height four and a-half inches, in diameter at top three and a-half inches. Around the upper part is a very rude ornamentation, formed by the usual mode of dotting in lines with some pointed instrument, per-

Urn found in a Barrow near the Boscawen-ûn Circle.

* I recently found a rude granite mortar, the very counterpart of the above, in an ancient circular work in the neighbouring parish of St. Paul.

direct to the Land's End. The cross at Crowz-an-wra was glanced at as we drove along. On the right were the hills of Chapel Carn Brea and Bartiné. An open country of cultivated fields, amidst tracts of moor and down, lay spread on the left and before us, until the long line of the distant horizon became visible, and approaching the cliffs we were soon as far westward as it was possible to go on England's soil.

St. Sennen Church.

It was scarcely archæological to pass St. Sennen's Church unheeded, but there was a long day's work before us; we had left Penzance an hour later than was originally intended, and as many of the company had never before

haps the end of a stick or a sharpened stone. At unequal distances the more numerous lines are crossed, but so carelessly as scarcely to form a regular pattern. Although of inferior workmanship, this little urn may be regarded with much interest on account of the locality in which it was found. By the kind permission of Miss Elizabeth Carne I am enabled to present the accompanying figure (see p. 191). Fragments of pottery also occurred at E, on the south-west side. The large rock with the cavity has long been known to the people of the neighbourhood as the "Money Rock."

visited the Land's End this was considered a favourable opportunity. Moreover, on the green turf lay spread white cloths bearing almost every kind of refreshment that could be brought to such a spot. This handsome luncheon had been provided by gentlemen of the neighbourhood, and as it was now near mid-day a halt of this sort was not unacceptable, for many had left Truro so early as six o'clock.

Here, on the dark cliffs of Bolerium, the British "Penrhyn Guard," the "promontory of blood," were assembled representatives of the Celtic races from Scotland, Wales, and Ireland, met on Cornish ground to investigate the monuments erected by their common forefathers centuries ago, erected in the ordinary course of a simple mode of life, by men little dreaming of a future in which the meaning of their cromlechs, tolmens, and circles could possibly become subjects for earnest controversy,—when the stones which they rudely heaped together to meet their commonest wants, and which are now the sole testimonies of their existence, should be regarded as objects of mystery,—when the greatest deeds of their best men should be forgotten, and not the name of one remembered.

The Land's End could not have been seen to greater advantage. There was a clear, bright sky overhead; the sun sent down cheering rays; the Atlantic was stretched out before us; the deep-blue waves were not angry, but they are never at rest; and the cliff-base and jutting rocks were fringed with snow-white foam. The old Longships looked as firm as ever, and we could see the cloud-like islands of Scilly breaking the line of the distant horizon. The company consisted of about a hundred, for many ladies and gentlemen from Penzance and neighbourhood had joined this day's excursion.

Leaving the Land's End, we again passed near St. Sennen's Church (see p. 192), but there was no time to enter it. It is a small, unattractive structure of the fifteenth century, interesting chiefly on account of an inscription on the stone at the base of the font, which, in the letters and with the usual abbreviations of the period, tells that "This church was dedicated on the festival of the Beheading of St. John the Baptist, A.D. 1441," and thus affording direct evidence of the date of the greater portion of the building; for it is not improbable that the walls of the chancel may have been erected long before. It was not unusual to re-dedicate a church when rebuilt or restored. The fifteenth-century piers shew much judgment in the use of that intractable granite; each presents a section of a square with three-quarter round shafts attached.

Section of Pier, St. Sennen Church.

About three o'clock we had arrived at the quaint old village of Treryn, and thence proceeded to the cliffs to examine the "castle" and the Logan Rock. This promontory was strongly fortified: three lines of circumvallation may still be traced. First, there is a broad ditch, A on the opposite plan, from the bottom of which to the summit of the first vallum of earth is about twelve feet. The second and third lines, B, C, appear to have been formed of masses of rock and earth, combined with the natural inequalities of the ground. They all extended to the sides of the cliffs as far as they were necessary; the cliffs themselves forming impenetrable barriers on the sea side. At D is another ditch cut across a narrow isthmus, and a straight light of defence exhibiting rude masonry. These are the remains of the finest cliff-castle in Cornwall, perhaps in England. Such structures were numerous on the coast of the Land's End district; almost every promontory was cut off in like manner. It is unnecessary to

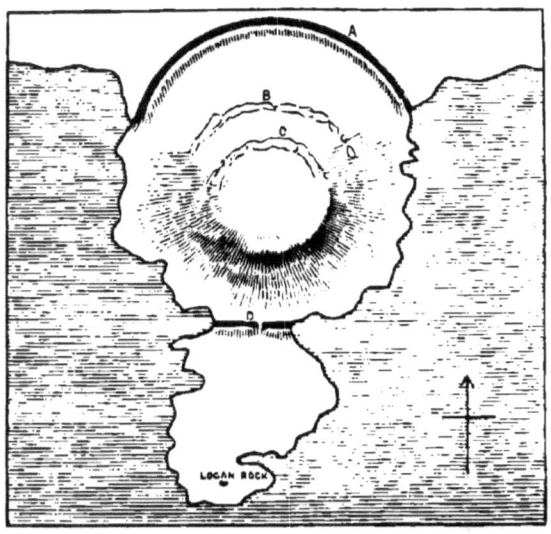

Plan of Castle Treryn.

repeat all the theories respecting their origin and use. Many have supposed them to be the works of the Danes, or other invading foes, who may have drawn up their ships in some sheltered cove hard by, fortified these promontories, and so gained a footing on the land, whereby they might at least so far subjugate the natives as to be able to procure for themselves necessary provisions. Before accepting this theory, however, it should be remembered that in many instances there are no landing-places near these fortifications, no sheltered coves in which to draw up boats, and the cliffs are altogether inaccessible. Supposing it possible for foreigners to have effected a landing and remained undisturbed sufficiently long to have constructed these fortifications, in all probability they would soon have been at the mercy of the natives. If shut up within their lines of defence their vessels could soon have been destroyed, unless there was a sufficient force without to protect them. If these invaders could not have been overcome in battle, supplies could have been withheld by the natives retiring inland with all their property. Indeed, there seems more reason to suppose these structures to have been the last strongholds of the natives themselves, driven seaward before a stronger race advancing on them from the east. The Rev. James Graves, the learned Secretary of the Kilkenny Archæological Society, who was present on this occasion, remarked at a subsequent meeting of the Kilkenny Society, that "The stone forts, cromlechs, caves, tumuli, and stone hut circles of the aborigines were alike in both countries (Ireland and Cornwall); but what chiefly attracted his attention was the fact that they were found clustered on the western hills and cliffs of England, just as we find them abounding on the western mountain sides and cliffs of Ireland. His impression was that the race which built them and fought in defence of them were a race fighting against an exterminating enemy; that they were unsuccessful; next found shelter in Ireland for a time, and were at last hurled over the cliffs of Kerry and Arran into the Atlantic. He defied any one to stand on the Cornish and the Kerry hills and not have the same idea forced on him." If the cliff-castles were the works of foreigners, it seems evident they must have been thorough masters of this part of the country.

The Logan Rock, a naturally formed rocking-stone, weighing above sixty tons, and poised on a grand pile of granite, was examined with interest by those to whom the locality was new.

Before the carriages had reached Treryn, a few members branched off to see St. Levan's Church. It has features

St. Levan's Church.

worthy of notice, but it was found impossible to include it among the objects to be visited in the day's excursion.

At St. Burian we had half-an-hour to examine the church, a large building of the fifteenth century. Remains of an earlier structure, however, exist in the chancel, which has in its north wall a Norman arch and pier with respond. The arch is built up, and the greater portion of the pier is buried in the masonry at the junction of the chancel with the east wall of the north aisle, but both are still distinctly

St. Burian Church.

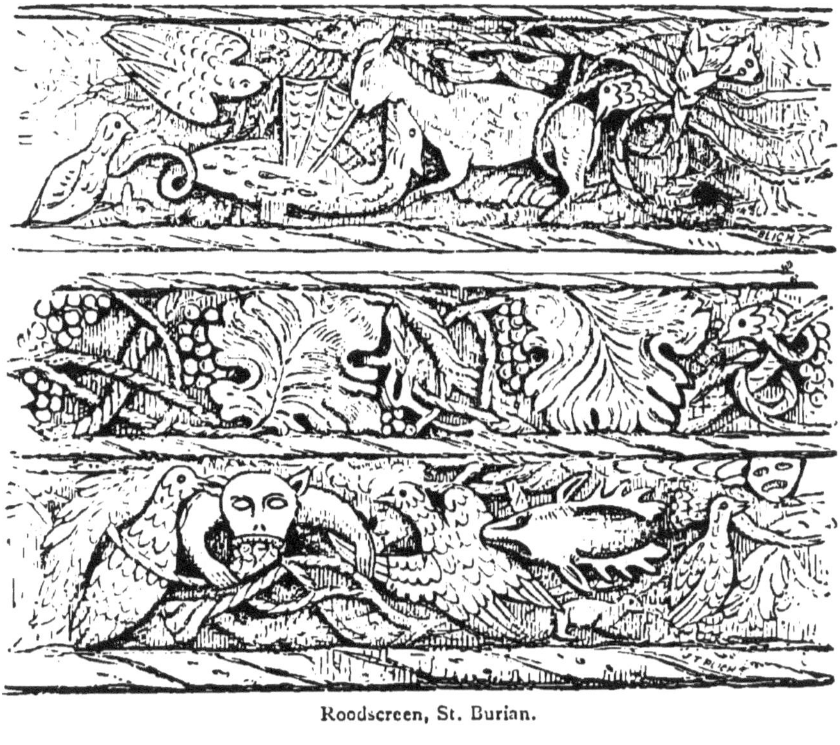

Roodscreen, St. Burian.

to be seen. The elaborately carved and painted roodbeam was much admired. The cross in the churchyard was not considered of very early date. Possibly it may be of the thirteenth or fourteenth century.

From St. Burian our route took a south-easterly course, passing on the road the Sanctuary cross. It is of the Latin form, and has the figure of our Lord dressed in a kilt carved in relief on one side. It still stands in the original socket-base, but a portion of the shaft has evidently been broken away. A quarter of a mile from this cross, beside a little stream on the farm of Bosliven, are the remains of an ancient structure called the Sanctuary. Athelstan is said to have founded the collegiate church of St. Burian, and to have granted to it the privilege of sanctuary. These ruins have been supposed to occupy the site of the original structure, but they are most probably no more than the walls of an oratory or chapel: buildings of this kind were numerous throughout Cornwall. It should be stated, however, that glebe lands had often, anciently, the privilege of sanctuary[b]. The people of the neighbourhood speak of the spot as the "Sentry." When I first went to see it no one could direct me to the "Sanctuary," but the site of the "Sentry" was well known. A correspondent of the GENTLEMAN'S MAGAZINE in 1781, after offering a few remarks on certain peculiarities in Cornish Churches, goes on to say:—

"I might add at the same time another circumstance which seems to me peculiar to the churches of Cornwall. There is in most parishes of this county a field (generally near the churchyard) which is commonly called the *sentry* (perhaps *sanctuary*), but this field is not always glebe land, or at least has been filched from the church in some in-

[b] See Dr. Petrie's Ecclesiastical Architecture of Ireland, &c.

stances. How came this name to be given to one field only in a parish? and why is not this field *always* glebe land?" In reference to the word *sentry*, the editor adds in a foot-note, " Probably *cemetery* (or burying-ground), as the old *cemetery*-gate at Canterbury is called by corruption *centry*-gate."—(Vol. li. p. 305.)

This enquiry of the correspondent of 1781 deserves more attention from Cornish archæologists than it appears to have received at the time. I have recently been informed that the two fields which constitute the glebe of St. Feock are known as the "Sentries," and the name is still probably retained in other parts of the county.

At Bolleit and Rosemoddress, adjoining estates, we had quite a cluster of interesting objects. First, there was the Rosemoddress circle, the "Dawns myin," consisting of nineteen stones; and by the roadside very near it a stone now used as a gate-post, measuring six feet in height, two feet seven inches as its greatest breadth, and nine inches thick, with a hole six inches in diameter pierced through it at the distance of one foot two inches from the upper edge.

In a gap in the hedge of a field on the opposite side of the road is a similar monument, four feet eight inches in length, and diminishing from two feet nine inches to ten inches in breadth. The hole, five and a-half inches in diameter, is seven and a-half inches from the edge of the broader end. It is about seven inches thick. I believe there is a third stone of like character at no great distance. They were all probably in some way connected with the circle. The Mên-an-tol in Madron parish, visited on the next day, seems to have formed one of the stones of a circle. Several holed stones of this description were found by the Rev. J. Buller near the circles at Carn Kenidzhek, in the parish of St. Just. (See Buller's "Account of the Parish of St. Just in Penwith," p. 100.) And in the parish of St. Constantine is a stone of triangular form with a large hole

Holed Stones, Bolleit.

through its centre. This latter stood near a barrow, and in later times a stone cross was erected near it. A cross yet stands by the roadside near one of the holed stones at Bolleit, and it is remarkable that a tolmen at Plymouth had a cross erected at a little distance from it. (See Davidson's "Notes on Antiquities of Devonshire.") It appears to have been the custom in early Christian days to set up the symbol of the cross where heathen rites prevailed. Indeed, superstitious practices connected with such stones are forbidden in Anglo-Saxon laws. (See Wilson's "Pre-Historic Annals of Scotland.") Holed stones of this description do not exist in Wales, though there are some in Scotland (see Toland's "History of the Celtic Religion"), and they are not unknown in Ireland.

A five minutes' walk from the holed stones brought us to two tall pillars of granite, one fifteen and a-half feet, the other thirteen and a-half feet high, and about three hundred yards asunder. They are popularly known as the "Pipers,"

The Pipers.

and resemble the menhirs of Wales and Brittany; as in the latter country, however, we do not find crosses placed on or incised in those stones. That they are sepulchral monuments there can be little doubt. A large urn was found beneath a similar pillar at Tresvannack, in the neighbouring parish of St. Paul. Tradition speaks of Bolleit as a battle-field, and that Athelstan here fought his last fight with the Cornu-Britons, and set up these monoliths as memorials of his victory. A few fields off stands another pillar ten feet high, and in the neighbourhood were numerous barrows, from which Hals says urns were taken.

At a few hundred yards' distance from the "Pipers," we came on what was considered of greater interest than anything else visited in the course of the day. This was the "Fogou" (Cornish, 'a cave'), a subterranean gallery with two smaller chambers. The principal passage is about thirty-six feet in length, four feet seven inches wide in the middle, diminishing to three feet three inches at the extremity; its greatest height is six feet two inches, the entrance (A) being the lowest part, only four feet two inches high. Five feet from the entrance on the left-hand side is an opening (B) with proper jambs and lintel, three feet high by eighteen inches wide; this leads to a chamber (C) about thirteen feet in length and four feet high: there is then another branch (D) about five feet in length, running nearly parallel to the first or principal gallery. All the sides are very rudely walled with unhewn stones built up without cement, and the roofs are formed of large slabs of granite thrown horizontally across. An opening has been made through the roof at the extremity of the main chamber. Through this nearly all the company passed. Learned archæologists descended to the proper entrance, were then lost to

Plan of the Fogou.

view for a few moments, and finally re-appeared at the opposite end, with different opinions as to the object of

Entrance to the Fogou.

this peculiar structure. Subterranean passages of this kind do not appear to exist in Wales, though Mr. Graves stated that he had seen similar ones in Ireland which were evidently used as places of concealment, for the chambers communicated one with the other most ingeniously. At the evening meeting Lord Dunraven said he had seen a great number of caves of this kind, and that it was very singular that forts nearly always possessed them. He had that day seen the remains of a fort around the cave the moment he looked for them. Dr. Simpson also referred to similar caves not far from Aberdeen. That this cave was surrounded by a fort there can be no doubt. Hals, describing this spot, says that in his time there was "still extant the downfalls of a castle or treble entrenchment, in the midst of which is a hole leading to a vault under ground. How far it extends no man now living can tell, by reason of the damps or thick vapours that are in it, for as soon as you go an arrow flight in it or less your candles will go out or extinguish of themselves for want of air." He then suggests that this was "probably an arsenal or store-house for laying up arms, ammunition, corn, and provisions." There are several caves of this description in Cornwall, some of them having numerous galleries branching off in a very intricate manner, and in all it will be observed that the entrances are extremely low and narrow; in no case is a doorway sufficiently high to admit a man unless he stoops or creeps through on hands and knees, though the chambers are not unfrequently more than six feet high. They vary in breadth, and the long galleries are generally curved; few continue in a straight line for any considerable distance. At Chapel Uny, in Sancreed parish, a narrow passage expands into a circular chamber, and then runs on again to the entrance of another. In some instances, as at Trewoofe and Trelowarren, are indications of these caves being surrounded by forts; from the peculiar positions of others, however, it is hard to believe that they could have been so enclosed.

Whilst the carriages were being driven to the top of Trewoofe (pronounced Trove) hill, many of the excursionists after leaving the Fogou crossed a little stream, climbed a prettily wooded bank, and then found themselves in front of the old manor-house of Trewoofe—or rather the house which occupies the site of the old building, of which the doorway alone remains. The jambs are richly sculptured with figures of men and other ornamentation, whilst above are carved the arms of the family of

Doorway, Trewoofe.

Levelis, or Leveale, viz., three calf's heads. Hals tells us that Leveale obtained Trewoofe in the time of Henry VIII.

through his marriage with the heiress of that name and house. A monument in St. Burian Church to Arthur Levelis of Trewoofe says:—

> "This worthy family hath flourished here,
> Since William's Conquest full six hundred year."

This Arthur Levelis, "last of his name," died in 1671. Mr. Levelis, who resided at Trewoofe during the time of the Great Rebellion, it is gratifying to know whilst on the spot, was a staunch Cavalier; and when, according to Hals, divers of the Royal party were pursued in the west by the troops under Fairfax, Mr. Levelis conveyed them to the "Fogou" which we have just inspected, and fed them until they found the opportunity to make their escape and join the King's party. The doorway, probably of the time of Henry VIII., is interesting, as shewing the style of work then bestowed on gentlemen's residences in this district; for it is rare to find at all in West Cornwall specimens of mediæval domestic architecture even of so late a date as this. We observed, however, many curious old cottages in St. Sennen church-town, rude and devoid of architectural character, but most probably as old as the church.

There was now nothing more to be visited: we were five miles from Penzance, which distance could not be driven over very rapidly, as we had to descend Newlyn-hill at a slow pace; affording time, however, to those who had not been in the neighbourhood before, to admire the beautiful views of Mount's Bay to be had from this locality.

A dinner at one of the principal hotels, and a meeting for the reading of papers and for remarks on the antiquities seen since the morning, concluded the day's proceedings.

On Friday, August 29, a company scarcely less numerous than that of the preceding day left Penzance about nine o'clock. Our course lay through the parish of Gulval, to the supposed British village of Chysauster, situated on the ridge and slope of a hill, the highest portion of which is occupied by the ancient fortification of Castle-an-dinas. The village with its surrounding enclosures extends over ten or twelve acres of ground, and there may still be traced the foundations of seven or eight huts, mostly of elliptical form; some are more circular than others, but all were constructed on the same principle. The accompanying plan shews the arrangement of one of them in a compara-

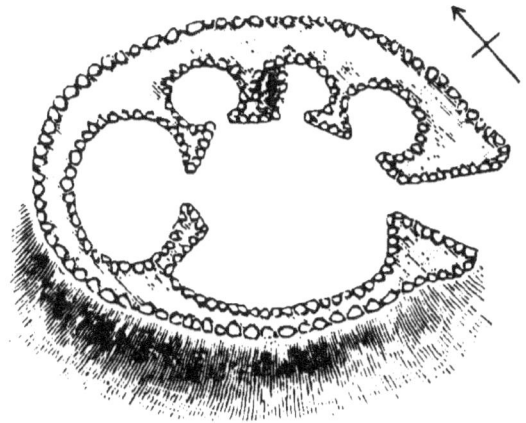

Plan of Hut, Chysauster.

tively good state of preservation. This is formed of a thick wall faced externally and internally with stones built together without cement, the intermediate space being filled with earth. On the north-east side, the highest part of the ground, the wall is about two feet high, and nine feet thick from the external facing to the small circular chambers. On the opposite side the wall is constructed on a rampart, sloping away from its base, and its height, exclusive of the rampart, is about nine or ten feet, the breadth four feet. The entrance faces a little east of south, and forms the approach to a passage somewhat more than twenty feet in length, and contracted in width towards the interior of the dwelling. Passing through this we came into a large open area thirty-two feet by thirty-four, from which openings led into small chambers apparently constructed within the thickness of the wall on the east and north sides. Three of these chambers are from fifteen to twelve feet in diameter; the fourth, opposite the entrance, being of much greater dimensions. One half of the second cell on the right of the entrance is deeper than the other. All these chambers are regularly walled; in some instances the stones appear to have been slightly overstepped, and thus gradually approaching as they increased in height, and giving the structure somewhat of a beehive form. The stone-work, however, does not appear to have converged sufficiently to have formed a perfect dome, and the apex of the roof was probably constructed of furze and turf laid on branches of trees. The large open area could only have been roofed by the erection of a pole in the centre, with others converging to its summit from the surrounding walls. No traces, however, of such construction exist, neither does it seem probable that this space was ever covered in. The dimensions of this hut are about eighty by sixty-five feet. Three or four yards north of this is another, somewhat less in size, on nearly the same plan: there are, however, but three cells, and the outer wall follows the shapes of those cells, not being carried around in a continuous curve as in that described above. This second hut has, within the large open area, two walled pits, each six by three feet, and similar in character, though much less in size, to those in the camp on Worle Hill in Somerset, and to those found in some of the Cornish hill-castles.

These two huts were connected by a bank of earth, and the whole cluster of dwellings extending over the hill slope were surrounded by enclosures of eccentric shapes. Beneath the dwellings, but still on the declivity of the hill, were two subterranean galleries, similar to that we entered at Bolleit. One was of considerable length, as may still be seen by the long trench and heaps of stones marking its site, for it has been utterly demolished by persons carrying away the larger stones for building purposes. The other, about a hundred yards distant, though partially destroyed, is sufficiently perfect to shew the mode of its construction, and resembles that at Pendeen, in St. Just, in having each course of stone overstepping that beneath. The roof was formed by long slabs of granite, as seen at Bolleit. Dr. Borlase dug up the floor of the Pendeen cave, but found little to repay the labour of his search, excepting a circular pit in one of the passages. Polwhele found ashes in one in the parish of St. Constantine, but no accompanying remains to afford a clue as to the period when the structure was formed. It has already been stated, in noticing the Bolleit Fogou, that caves of this kind occur within ancient fortifications. Polwhele, in his "Historical Views of Devon," refers to one at South Huish, near an entrenchment on the declivity of a hill, and Borlase describes another at Bodinnar, in the parish of Sancreed, in Cornwall, which spot, from the numerous heaps of stones and traces of hut circles, he considers to be the site of a British town. Many writers have considered those structures to have been store-chambers, and as places of refuge in times of danger. Some have even conjectured that they were used as habitations—dwelling-places of the natives of the country! But any one who has ever inspected them must admit that they are altogether unsuited to be places of abode, though it is not improbable, as in the instance of the party of Royalists at Bolleit, that they may have been temporarily occupied as hiding-places. It seems to be clearly ascertained that in this country some primitive races did at times live in caves, and have left traces of such habitation, as, for instance, at Kent's Hole at Torquay; but this, and all other caves which were occupied as dwelling-places, were as different as possible from the Fogous, the long, walled, subterranean chambers of Cornwall.

The Cornish caves are perhaps akin to the "Giants' Chambers" and "earth-houses" of Norway, Sweden, and the Highlands of Scotland; and to the "passage-buildings" described by Worsaae in his "Primeval Antiquities of Denmark." Many appear to have been formed in such situations as to render them difficult to be discovered, and to the present day the people have superstitions respecting those caves, that it is dangerous to enter them, and that some near the coast run long distances under the sea. That at Bodinnar was called the "Giant's Holt," and, Borlase says, has "no other use at present than to frighten and appease forward children." Of the Bolleit cave it is said that the roof will fall in and crush any one who remains there more than a certain number of minutes. All these superstitious notions may at least be considered good evidence of the antiquity of these peculiar structures, and it appears that similar tales are attached to the "earth-houses" of Denmark, as may be seen by the following quotation from Robert Jamieson's "Illustrations of Northern Antiquities:"—

"'Earth-houses,' as they were called, were built underground in hillocks, the entrance to which, being concealed by trees and underwood, was known only to those to whom they belonged. Here plate, jewels, armour, or whatever was more precious, was deposited for security against any sudden invasion, such as they were continually exposed to; and those who were interested in preventing the places from being explored industriously propagated reports of its being the retreat of a *Drac* (demon) of the most malignant and terrible description. Every chief had his peculiar cavern, treasury, or hiding-place, which was known only to those whom it most concerned. Caverns of this kind are everywhere pointed out at this day in Norway, Sweden, and the Highlands of Scotland; and if they are but sufficiently large and dark, never without some terrible story of the dragon or demon who was encountered by the warrior, harper, or bag-piper who, in quest of the treasure, ventured too far."

If the Cornish caves were thoroughly investigated with

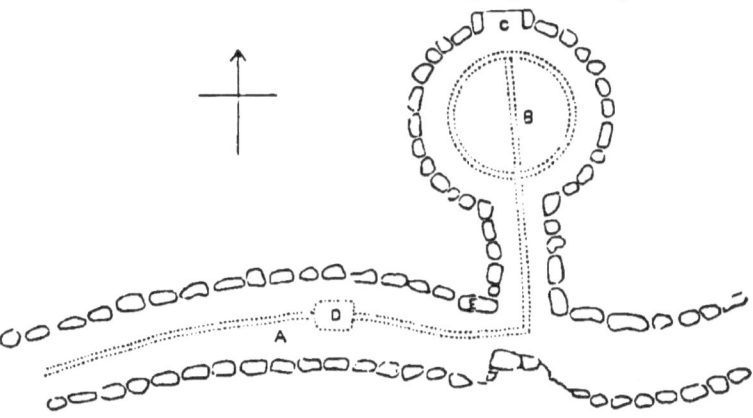

Plan of Cave, Chapel-Uny.

great care, no doubt something might be found to afford a clue to their origin and purpose. The Chapel-Uny cave

Cornish Antiquities.

in the parish of Sancreed—alluded to in the account of the preceding day's excursion—has recently been partially explored. In opening it, it was found that the long passage (A on the plan), thirty-five feet in length, was filled to the roof with soil, in many places much discoloured. The circular chamber B—perhaps unique as regards the Cornish caves, though a similar arrangement occurs at the Picts' House at West Grange of Conan, Forfarshire—was undoubtedly a perfect dome or bee-hive-shaped cell entirely constructed of stone, about ten or twelve feet high, and with a diameter of fifteen feet. At C is a recess with jambs and lintel, measuring in height two feet seven inches, in breadth three feet one inch, in depth two feet. The circular chamber was not found to have been filled with earth—at least it contained nothing more than the *débris* of the fallen roof. On reaching the floor it was discovered that drains regularly constructed of stone were carried through the midst of each chamber, as indicated by the dotted lines on the plan. The drain through the long gallery leads into a deeper pit at D^c.

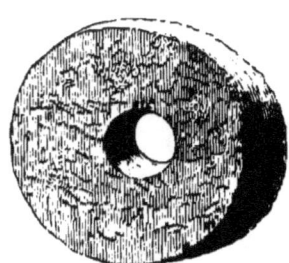

Stone Amulet, from Cave, Castle-Uny.

^c These drains are not now visible, but for information respecting their positions I am indebted to Mr. W. C. Borlase, who has in his possession the few relics discovered during the exploration of the cave. I engrave, by Mr. Borlase's permission, what appears to be a stone amulet, about one inch in diameter. It was taken from behind the large granite block (E) to the right of the entrance to the long chamber. There were also found fragments of pottery, one piece very like Samian ware, an article resembling an iron spear-head, and another of the form of a large fish-hook.

The " Giants' Chambers" of Denmark were filled up like the passage in this structure. Worsaae says the "circular chambers, and even the entrances, which are from sixteen to twenty feet in length, are filled with trodden earth and pebbles, the object of which doubtless was to protect the repose of the dead in their grave." He suggests that they had been thus filled as soon as a corpse had been deposited, " and not to have been opened until a new corpse was to be interred [d]."

Above the Chysauster cave the hill-side is scarped into a succession of terraces, each platform being very evenly levelled. The ground was so thickly overgrown with furze and brambles as to prevent our entering many of the hut-dwellings, but two of the best examples were inspected with interest [e].

Leaving Chysauster, we had to proceed through a rather rough lane to a place called New Mill, where we got on the high road from Penzance to Zennor, and passing under Mulfra Hill, crowned with a cromlech, of which we had a distant view, we drove over the Zennor Down towards the village of Treryn. All the company, however, did not proceed to the latter place, for we stopped on the way, and it was explained that those who wished to inspect a beehive hut at Bosphrennis, which had been brought into notice only a few weeks previously by Mr. Thomas Cornish, might do so by walking about a mile across the Down, and that carriages would be driven round and be kept in waiting for them as near as they could be brought to the Bos-

[d] Worsaae's Primeval Antiquities of Denmark, translated by W. J. Thoms.

[e] In vol. xviii. of the Archæological Journal I have given a plan of the whole village of Chysauster, with illustrations of masonry, &c.

phrennis village. Fifteen or sixteen gentlemen availed themselves of this arrangement, and did not afterwards regret having taken this special excursion. About three or four hundred yards from the road we saw the remains of a circle which appeared to have consisted of numerous upright pillars, with rude masonry between them. This is probably the Zennor circle of Borlase. Between this spot and the Mulfra cromlech, as well as on the route to Bosphrennis, are several barrows, some of which have been opened.

The Bosphrennis hut has already been so ably described

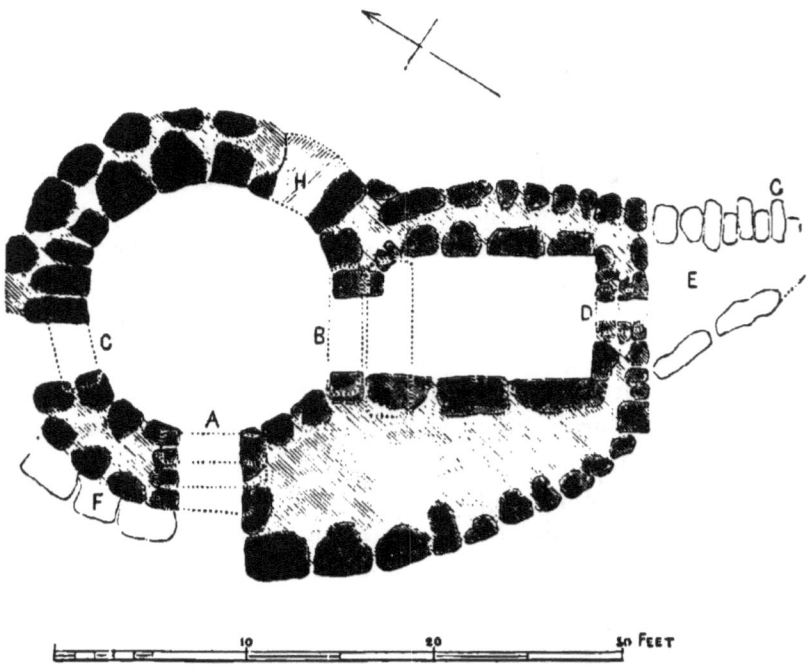

Plan of Bee-hive Hut, Bosphrennis.

by the Rev. E. L. Barnwell in the *Archæologia Cambrensis* that little need be said beyond what is necessary to explain the accompanying illustrations. The hut consists of two chambers, one circular, thirteen feet in diameter, the other rectangular, nine by seven feet; with a communicating doorway, B on the plan, measuring four feet high

Fig. 1. Fig. 2.
Sections of Masonry, Bee-hive Hut, Bosphrennis.

by three feet nine inches in breadth. The principal entrance, A, five feet six inches high and two feet wide, has a lintel composed of three slabs of granite. C marks another entrance only two feet seven inches high and two feet three inches wide; one lintel stone remains, but there were evidently others, for the outer facing of the wall on this side has suffered much injury, many of the stones having been carried away. At H the wall has been broken through, thus affording a good section, and shewing the mode of construction. All the stones—large blocks of

Exterior of End of Rectangular Chamber, Bee-hive Hut, Bosphrennis.

granite—used in this structure appear to have been selected with much care. In the circular chamber each course overlaps that beneath, the stones at the height of five feet projecting inwardly three feet beyond those at the base, as shewn by fig. 1 in the woodcut opposite, and appear to have thus continued until a perfect dome was formed; the roof has fallen in, and the present height of the wall is from five to six feet. The masonry over the doorway, B, is stepped over towards both chambers (see fig. 2), but the remaining three sides of the rectangular one consists of perpendicular walling to the height of seven feet without shewing any indication of the manner in which the roof was formed. It was thought at first that the rectangular chamber was of later date, but on more careful examination this was not found to be the case, and there can be no doubt that the whole building was constructed at the same time. In the end of the rectangular chamber, five feet from the ground, is a small window, which, as regards structures of this kind, Mr. Barnwell considers to be unique in England and Wales:—

"For although Tref Caeran in Caernarvonshire may still retain a doorway in the outer defences, yet no other instance of a window is known. Even in the more numerous and perfect specimens of such buildings in the west of Ireland (for an excellent account of which see Mr. Dunoyer's article in the Archæological Journal, vol. xv.) only one window is figured in Plate IV. of the article referred to, and it appears to have been much more carefully and neatly executed than the one at Bosphrennis [1]."

The masonry of the side walls of the inner chamber appears to have been executed with much greater care and regularity than the end in which the window occurs. At F and E are low platforms about eighteen inches in height, and at G three steps in the hedge. The use of these platforms is not apparent, neither is it evident what purpose the great thickness of the south-west wall could have served. On the opposite side, it will be observed, the wall externally follows the shape of the chambers, whilst here there is, to all appearance, a solid mass of earth between

[1] *Archæologia Cambrensis*, Third Series, No. xxxiv.

Cornish Antiquities.

Entrance to Circular Chamber, Bee-hive Hut, Bosphrennis.

Interior of Circular Chamber, Bee-hive Hut, Bosphrennis.

the two facings. At present there is not known to exist in Cornwall any other building of the period to which this is assigned to be compared with it. The interesting bee-hive huts of Roughtor and Brown Willy described by Sir Gardner Wilkinson are of a different character. One of the gentlemen present stated that if he had seen this building of a round and rectangular chamber in Ireland he should have called it an oratory—a place in which some religious man established himself and had a little chapel attached. Whatever may have been its use, the striking resemblance of this building to those in Ireland seems to afford another proof of the connexion which existed between the two countries at an early period. This bee-hive hut stands in the angle of a small enclosure, the hedges of which are built of the stones which at one time formed other similar structures, and which were destroyed by a former tenant, but within the remembrance of the person now occupying the estate. In an adjoining field are the remains of the foundations of rectangular chambers surrounded by a rudely constructed circle, and at a distance of a few hundred yards, among furze and heath, are traces of circular enclosures resembling those at Chysauster.

After having examined the bee-hive hut, we retraced our steps through a few fields to the side of a little stream, the course of which we followed for a short distance, then directed our way to a croft on the left, and came on the fallen cromlech of Bosphrennis. It consisted of four supporters three feet six inches high, forming a complete kist-vaen six feet by three, and what is very remarkable, the covering-stone is circular, measuring four feet ten inches in diameter and five inches thick. The stone must certainly have been wrought into this form, and it seems to afford the only known instance of the kind. It was suggested that it was made circular in modern times,—in fact, that

Fallen Cromlech, Bosphrennis.

the cromlech was pulled down for this stone,—and that after it had been shaped it was found useless for the purpose required. But, after all, it scarcely seems likely that any one would be at the labour of rounding a large piece of granite without first ascertaining whether it was of suitable dimensions and quality. Though—owing to the rough character of the intervening ground—we had to proceed on a roundabout course, this cromlech is no more than about five hundred yards from the bee-hive hut.

It was but a short walk to the conveyance which had been left behind for us. We had now a good sea view, and just below could see the situations of the Gurnard's Head and Bosigran, both fortified headlands. After proceeding nearly parallel with the coast for a mile or two our route took an inland direction, and we soon came in sight of

Chûn-hill, and at a mile distant could perceive that the castle was already in the possession of the advanced party of our forces.

Approaching the hill from the north-east we first passed through the hut-dwellings of Bosullow, about a furlong from the castle. These, as will be seen by the annexed plan,

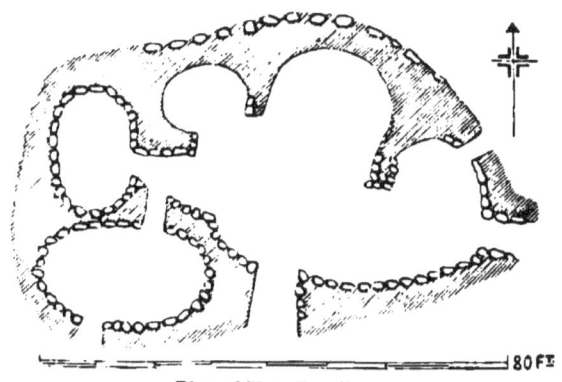

Plan of Hut, Bosullow.

are very similar in arrangement to those at Chysauster, each enclosure containing three or four small chambers with an open area. Since our visit a few excavations have been made here. I have been informed that a quern was found, and have seen that a considerable amount of wood-ashes were dug up from under the turf which had overgrown the floors, thus shewing that those enclosures were at some period the habitations of man. There appears to have been a protected roadway from the huts to the castle. This we followed, and ascending to the summit of the hill, entered within the ruined walls of Chûn Castle, where we found a handsome luncheon—as on the preceding day provided by gentlemen of the neighbourhood—spread on

Cornish Antiquities. 223

cloths on the smooth turf. As those who had first arrived had been waiting for the Bosphrennis party, no further delay was now necessary. The proceedings of the following hour need not be narrated to those who have enjoyed a picnic on an interesting spot on a fine summer's day. A few speeches were made—Cornish gentlemen welcoming the members of the Association, and the members in return expressing their thanks for the hearty and kind manner in which they had been received and entertained.

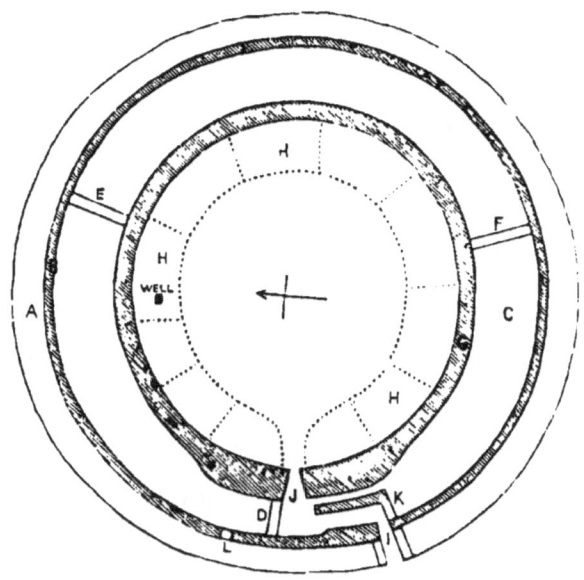

Plan of Chûn Castle.

Chûn Castle has been greatly mutilated, large quantities of the stone having been carried away and used in the erection of modern buildings. Its plan and arrangement can, however, be still distinctly traced, and some portions of the walls retain good examples of the masonry. The castle consisted of two ditches and two strongly-built concentric walls. The first ditch, A on the plan, is twenty feet wide. The wall B, five or six feet thick, is now from six to seven feet in height in some parts, but Dr. Borlase says it was at least ten feet in height. The second ditch, C, rather more than thirty feet wide, is divided by transverse walls, D, E, F. The wall G, twelve feet thick, Dr. Borlase considers to have been originally not less than fifteen feet high. Within this wall is an open area, one hundred and eighty feet by one hundred and seventy. This, however, appears to have contained a third concentric wall of less strength, and about twenty-five feet from the wall G, the intervening space being divided by partitions radiating from the centre of the building into several compartments, H, H, H : in one of which, on the north side, is a well, described by Dr. Borlase as regularly walled around and having steps descending to the water.

These compartments are described by Britton in his "Beauties of England and Wales," and by Cotton in the fifteenth volume of the *Archæologia* of the Society of Antiquaries, as of circular form. But there can be little doubt that Dr. Borlase was correct in his plan, which in this particular agrees with that accompanying this paper. This arrangement shews a striking similarity between the ground-plans of this, a British work, and the Norman castle of Restormel, also in Cornwall. In the latter the apartments are between two concentric walls, and have their entrances from the circular open area. It would seem, therefore, that the builders of the later circular castles of Cornwall borrowed their ground-plans from older works. The entrance I, through the outer wall, faces south-west. From this a passage, thirty-eight feet long, leads to the entrance J through the second wall G. Between this passage and the wall G is another, only three feet in breadth, and communicating with that division of the ditch between the transverse walls K, F. The entrance J splays outwardly to a considerable degree; at the inner part, where two jambs about five feet in height remain, it is six feet wide, whilst the broadest part measures sixteen feet. From the left side of this entrance a wall extended towards the outer one, B. The extreme thickness of the wall on each side of the entrance J is remarkable. It will be observed that the outer wall was strengthened in like manner on one side of the entrance I. If of no other use, this extraordinary breadth would have served for a great number of warriors to stand on the walls and defend their entrances from attacking forces. There seems to have been another entrance at L; the wall here is much mutilated, but the sides of this opening look as if they had been regularly faced. The masonry is much superior to that found in the Cornish hill-castles; indeed, it shews considerable skill in the construction of a large building with dry-stone work. The outer wall at the right hand of the entrance I presents a good specimen of the masonry, and it will be seen by the annexed cut that the stones were placed with much regularity and care.

Masonry of Outer Wall, Chûn Castle.

The castle and huts at Bosullow are probably of the same period. The former would always have afforded a place of refuge for the inhabitants of the latter in case of attack from invaders or hostile tribes.

The hill-side is studded with numerous small barrows, and five or six hundred yards west of the castle stands the Chûn Cromlech, consisting of four supporters and covering

Chûn Cromlech.

stone forming a rectangular kistvaen. It was surrounded by a circle of stones, some of which still remain. These formed perhaps the base of a mound which may have covered the cromlech. Of course it is doubtful whether it ever was thus buried, for there is no mound hard by formed of the soil which would have been thrown off. The supposition that such a heap would have disappeared in the lapse of ages scarcely applies in this case, for, as already stated, the hill side is studded with small barrows, not a quarter of the height necessary to contain this cromlech, yet they remain apparently just as they were when first constructed. Surely if the material which formed a mound eight or ten feet high was dispersed through exposure or through some inexplicable process connected with time, how much more rapidly should the lesser mounds have disappeared. If mounds over cromlechs were wilfully removed for the sake of pillaging the kistvaens, how comes it that those kistvaens themselves are not demolished? It does not seem likely that the depredators who destroyed the mounds would have much respect for the stone chambers. Such are some of the difficult points for consideration in connexion with this question. Good evidence has been brought forward that certain cromlechs were covered with barrows; in fact, that this was the case in many instances admits of no doubt, but some perhaps were merely surrounded by circles of stones. It is remarkable that structures very similar to our cromlechs are now in use among the natives of India. Mr. W. J. Henwood has described those Indian cromlechs in the Reports of the Royal Institution of Cornwall. Indeed, the form of this monument admits of its being used for many purposes, though there can be no doubt that those existing in countries occupied by Celtic tribes were constructed as sepulchral chambers.

The next objects to be seen were the Mên Scryfa and the Mên-an-tol. We soon came to the road leading to them; it was, however, found to be too rough to be driven over, so leaving the carriages we started on a walk, the Mên Scryfa being about half-a-mile distant. It is a rough granite pillar, seven feet two inches high, and bears the inscription, RIALOBRAN-CUNOVAL-FIL, the letters running lengthways of the stone, which is always the case in the earliest inscribed stones of Cornwall. This monument is supposed to be of the fifth or sixth century.

On our way back across the moor we visited the Mên-an-tol. This curious monument, as its name implies, is a stone with a hole through it. It stands between two others, at the distance of seven feet ten inches from one

Mên-an-tol, Madron.

and seven feet eight inches from the other. A few yards north-west of the westernmost stone are two others, one fallen the other upright; and it seems probable that these are the only remaining stones of a circle. The holed stone is three feet six inches high by four feet three inches in breadth at base. The hole measures in diameter on one side two feet two inches, on the other one foot seven inches. One side may have been bevelled for some particular purpose, or perhaps is the result of the hole having been made with a rude instrument worked only on one side of the stone. The hole of the Tolven, in the parish of St. Constantine, is bevelled in like manner. Superstitious practices have been observed at these stones in modern times. Dr. Borlase has referred to such customs. Children were passed through the Mên-an-tol as a cure for spinal diseases, and some amusement was afforded at the time of our visit by several of the excursionists creeping through the hole.

It was but a short stage in our journey from the Mên-an-tol to the Lanyon cromlech. This monument stands on the top of a hill, and has three supporting stones, each about five feet high, and a covering-stone seventeen feet four inches long by eight feet nine inches as its greatest breadth, and weighing about nine tons. The covering-stone was thrown down during a violent thunder-storm in the year 1816, and replaced in 1824. The Lanyon cromlech has therefore lost much of the interest which would otherwise have been attached to it had it still stood as when first erected. The supporting stones in their present position could not have formed a rectangular kistvaen, neither do they appear as if they had been intended for the sides of a circular chamber, as is sometimes the case in monuments of this kind. Probably these stones were shifted when the cap-stone was replaced, and other supporting stones may have existed, though it is remarkable that many cromlechs possess only three. A cromlech at Caerwynen, in Cornwall, has three only, and it is well known that the frequent occurrence of this arrangement in some localities has caused certain antiquaries to class them under the name of *triliths*, though these are now generally considered to be the mere ruins of more complicated structures. About a furlong from the Lanyon cromlech, in the midst of a sloping field, are the remains of another, which we did not visit. The covering-stone, eighteen feet eight inches long, and a supporting stone, five feet nine inches high, still exist. This cromlech is particularly worthy of notice, because it afforded proof that monuments of its class were sometimes buried under mounds. It appears that a gentleman who owned the estate happening to notice the mound, and remarking that the soil appeared to be very rich, sent his servants to remove it. When they had taken away about a hundred cart-loads they observed the supporting stones of a cromlech, from which the covering-stone had slipped off. Digging beneath the stones they found a broken urn and ashes, with half a skull, the thigh bones, and most of the other bones of a human body. From the position of these remains, however, it appeared that the cromlech had been previously opened. An account of this discovery is given in vol. xiv. of the *Archæologia* of the Society of Antiquaries.

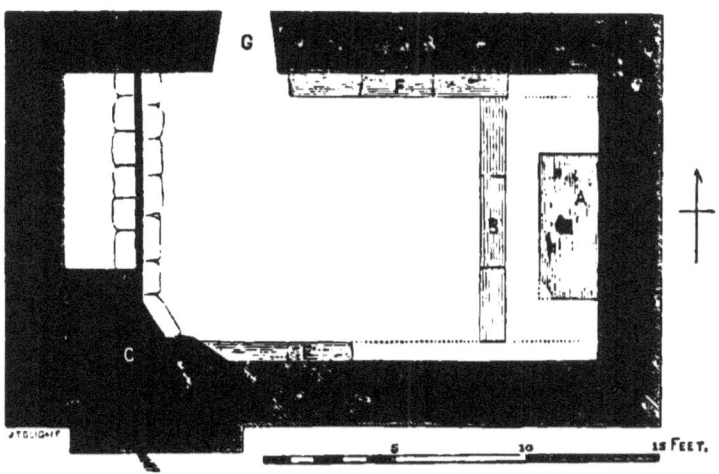

Plan of St. Madron's Well.

St. Madron's Well was not placed on the programme of the day's excursion, but when we reached the road leading to it, it was found that we had half-an-hour to spare, so leaving the carriages, we walked about a furlong over a low marshy tract until we came to the roofless walls of the little building, measuring internally twenty feet four inches by eleven feet, with walls a little more than two feet thick. In the east end is the *mensa* of the altar, A in the plan, with a mortice sunk in its midst, probably for the reception of a crucifix or image of the saint. A row of flat stones, B, one foot four inches from the altar, divides the sanctuary from the nave. In the south-west corner of the latter is the well, C, four feet six inches by two feet ten inches, the superstructure being about four feet high, and roofed by each course of stone being made to overlap. The work is somewhat irregular, but the builders have managed by the use of stone alone—commencing on a rectangular base— to form the upper part into a rude dome-shaped cell. This well was supplied from a little perennial stream which flows within a few feet of the south wall. The water was let in through a properly-constructed opening in the wall at D, and when it overflowed the pit ran out at E, whence a channel conducted it on to the opposite side of the building, where it appears to have been allowed to percolate under the wall, for outside this wall there was no drain, though one has been made there within the last three months. The labourers who constructed the present drain informed me that they found no remains of a former one. It appears, therefore, to have been the custom to fill the well-pit, and then stop the supply of water from the running stream. Stone benches, F, F, were built against the two side walls; the upper stones were wrought to a smooth surface, and being of greater breadth than the masonry beneath, their under edges were bevelled by a plain chamfer.

The doorway G in the north wall splays inwardly, measuring two feet without, two feet eight inches within. This baptistery was enclosed by an outer wall, the foundations of which may yet be traced.

St. Madron's was the most celebrated of the holy wells of Cornwall: remarkable cures are said to have been effected by virtue of its waters. Norden says, "Its fame in former ages was greate for the supposed virtue of healinge which St. Maderne had thereinto infused." Bishop Hall, in "The Invisible World," gives an instance of the miraculous cure of a poor cripple by resorting to this well. Even at the present time many of the poorer people seem to believe in the efficacy of this water, for on the first three Sundays in May they take their sickly children to the baptistery that they may be strengthened and cured by immersion. After the visitation of these votaries small pieces of rag and bandages will be found fastened to the surrounding bushes—a practice also observed in connexion with the holy wells of Scotland and Ireland.

After leaving Chûn Castle, some of the excursionists preferred going on to see St. Madron's Church instead of walking to the Mên Scryfa and Mên-an-tol. Those who visited the church seem to have found in it some points of interest, and Mr. E. A. Freeman favoured those present with remarks on its architecture. Illustrations of the sedile, piscina, font, and other details are given above, pp. 24—31.

We arrived at Penzance in good time for the train by which the members of the Association were to proceed to Truro for the evening meeting. At this meeting, as on the previous day, Professor Babington gave a most instructive account of the numerous objects visited, referring more particularly to Chûn Castle and to the Bosphrennis Bee-hive hut.

This, the sixteenth meeting of the Association, was formally dissolved on Saturday, August 30, but a few of the members remained behind, and early in the following week ventured across the sea over the submerged tract of Lyonesse to the Scilly Islands, where they were hospitably received by the proprietor, Mr. Augustus Smith. To interest the visitors it was proposed to open a barrow on the island of Samson. I borrow the following from an interesting account of the investigation written by Mr. Smith, and published in the Reports of the Royal Institution of Cornwall :—

"The workmen employed first excavated a passage about four feet wide, beginning from the exterior circle which constitutes the outer base of the round, and carefully keeping in their progress to the level or surface of the natural ground. The mound in its outer circumference measured about fifty-eight yards, giving therefore a distance of nearly thirty feet to its centre. For about eighteen or twenty feet the mound appeared entirely composed of fine earth, when an inner covering first of smaller and then of larger rugged stones was revealed. These were carefully uncovered before being disturbed, and were then one by one displaced till a large upright stone was reached, covered by another of still more ponderous dimensions. This top covering, measuring about seven feet six inches in its largest diameter, was found to be the lid of a chamber beneath, in which was discovered part of an upper jaw-bone, presenting the alveolæ of all the incisors, the canines, and three molars, and the roots of two teeth, very white, still remaining in their sockets. Another fragment gave part of the lower jaw with similar remains of teeth in the sockets. All the bones had been under the action of fire, and must have been carefully collected together after the burning of the body, to have been found placed as they were[g]. They are con-

[g] When the relics taken out of this grave were exhibited at the late meeting of the Cornwall Institution, there was found with the bones a curious double-edged piece of stone, designated a *flint-flake*.

Kistvaen, Samson, Scilly.

sidered to have belonged to a man about fifty years of age. The bottom of the sarcophagus was neatly fitted with a pavement of three flat but irregular-shaped stones, the joints fitted with clay mortar, as were also the interstices where the stones forming the upright sides joined together, as also of the lid, which was very neatly and closely fitted down with this same plaster, shewing most clearly it never could have been disturbed from the time it had been first constructed. Two long slabs, from seven to nine feet in length and two feet in depth, form the sides, while the short stones fitted in between them make the ends, being about three and a-half feet apart, and to fix which firmly in their places, grooves had been roughly worked in the larger stones."

This grooving of the stones is remarkable, proving that implements of some kind were occasionally employed on monuments of this period, and rendering it a not very improbable case that the covering-stone of the Bosphrennis cromlech was worked to its present circular form when first erected.

There can be no doubt that for the moment the visit of the Cambrian Association excited a revival in the interest of Cornish antiquities, and there is reason to hope it may be maintained.

It is in the power of the Cornish Societies to do much towards the promotion of further research, and the preservation of the antiquities of the county. For the latter, however, aid should be more particularly looked for from the landholders. If the stewards and agents of gentlemen having land in Cornwall were to impress on the tenants that certain structures were not to be meddled with, it would surely to some extent be the means of preventing their wilful destruction.

In the official report of the Truro Meeting of the Cambrian Association it is stated that the Land's End district " stands unrivalled in any portion of Europe of the same extent as regards the value and variety of its monuments." Certainly there is not in Cornwall another district possessing so many objects of antiquarian interest so thickly clustered; but the whole of the county is still a good field for archæological research. There are outlying tracts to be examined and reported on, affording work for those who really care for the subject for many years to come.

INDEX OF PLACES,

With Reference to Engravings denoted by an Asterisk.

ANTHONY in Kirrier, St., 77—81; parish church, legend of foundation of, 78; general view of church, 79*; windows of chancel and aisle, 80; font, 81*; cusps of window, 176; window, 176*.
Austell, St., tower of, 162.

Bolleit, holed stones, 201; the Pipers, 202*; the Fogou, 203*; entrance to the Fogou, 204*.
Boscawen-ûn-Circle, 188*; plan of barrow near, stone found in, 190*, 191*; urn found in, 191*.
Bosliven, "the Sanctuary," 14, 199.
Bosphrennis, Bee-Hive hut, plan of, 215*; sections of masonry of, 216*; exterior of end of rectangular chamber, 217*; entrance to circular chamber, interior of circular chamber, 219*; fallen cromlech, 221*.
Bosullow, hut, plan of, 222*.
Breage, St., 109—114; "Bishop Rock," 111; helmet, 112*; "hill-castle," 112; capitals, 113*; head of cross, 114*; shallow transept, 168; porch, 177; ornament, 180.
Burian, St., oratory of, Athelstan founds college at, 2; deanery of, 1—24; "church town" of, 5; church, 5; font, 6*; roodscreen and benches, 7; arcades and cornice of roodscreen, 7*; spiral staircase, 8; misereres, 9*; chancel, piscina, and aisles, 10; capital and base of pier, 10*; tomb of Clarice de Bolleit, 11, 12*; tower, bells, 12; porch, church property, ancient crosses, 13, 14; turret, 173*; porch, 177, 178*; capitals, 179; general view of church, roodscreen, 198*.

Camborne, 158, 159; symbols of the five wounds, 159*.
Castle Treryn, plan of, 195*.
Chapel Uny, cave at, 205; plan of, 212*; stone amulet found in, 213*.
Chûn Castle, plan of, 223*; masonry of outer wall, 225*; cromlech, 226*.
Chysauster, British village at, 208, 214; plan of, 208*.
Crowan, St., 158.
Cury, 45—49; south doorway, 46*; nave, windows, and aisles, 47; hagioscope, 47; plan of hagioscope, 48*; low side window, 49*.

Eglos-Berrie, named after St. Burian, 2.
Erth, St., 128; window of north aisle, 128*; stringcourse of tower, 129*; window, 176*.

Index of Places.

Germoe, St., 114—120; general view of church, 115*; gable cross of porch, gable corbels of porch, 117*; font, 118*; St. Germoe's chair, 119*; shallow transept, 168; panelled pinnacles, 170.
Goldsithney, St. James' Chapel at, 124.
Gothian's, St., Oratory, 138*, 163, 164.
Grade, St., 97.
Gulval, St., 124—127; credence, pinnacle of tower, 125*; tower-arch, 126*; shields on font, 127*.
Gunwalloe, 50—54; the cove, 50; general view of church, 50*; bells, open roof, 52, 53; fragment of font, 54*; epitaph in churchyard, 54; window and cusp, 175*; capital, 181*.
Gwinear, St., 130—136; plan of church, 131*; chancel window, 132*; piscina, beak-head, corbel-heads, 133*; font, 134; symbol of sacred wound, 135*; general view of church, 169*; tower, one of loftiest in Cornwall, 172.
Gwithian, St., 136, 137; transept, 136*; plan of St. Gothian's oratory, 138*; doorway, 139*; Porth-curnow Chapel, 141*; panelled pinnacle, 170.

Hilary, St., 156, 157; blocked spire-light, tower, 157*, 172, 173.

Ives, St., ancient name of, 1; description of church, 142—148; shields on panels of seat, section of pier, pier-arch moulding, 143*; chancel roof, 144*; arched recess, 144; tower, 145, 162; font, 145*; bench standard, 147*.

Just in Penwith, St., 40—43, 159; capitals, 41; hoodmould, tooth-moulding, 42*; windows, 42; tower and bells, 43; inscribed stone, 43*; discoveries made at, 159; pinnacle, 170*; window, 176*.

Keverne, St., 60—66; capital and base of pier, 63*; plan of church, 64*; shields on bench-ends, 65*; font, monument in north aisle, 66; spire, 173.

Landewednack, 82—88; plan of church, 82*; low side window, 83*; boss on porch, 84*; south doorway, 85*; font, inscription on, 86*; founder's marks on bells, 87*.
Lelant, 129, 130; capital and base of Norman pier, 130*.
Levan, St., 15—21; arched doorway, 16; stoup, 16*; bench-ends, 17*; monogram, 17*; transept, 18*, 19*; capitals of pier, 19*; font, 20*; woodwork of roof, 20; tower, ancient crosses, well, and chapel, 20, 21; impost, 180*; general view of church, 197*.
Ludgvan, granite of, best for fine work, 6; description of church, 127; panelled pinnacles, 170; crockets, 178.

Madron, St., 24—31; font, 26*; sedile and piscina, 27*; aisles, rood-screen, tower, 28, 29; corbel-table and window of tower, 29*; figures of archangels, 30*; mural monuments, 30; epitaph on George Daniel, parish registers, 31; baptistery, 163; Mên-an-tol, 228*; Lanyon cromlech,

229; plan of St. Madron's well, 230*.
Manaccan, 67—72; plan of church, piscina in transept, 67*; interior of chancel, 68*; south-east view of chancel and transept, 69*; south doorway. 70*; tower, 71; Early English work at, 167.
Mawgan in Kerrier, St., 72—77; hagioscope, 72*; effigies, 74*; shields on tower, keystones of tower-window and tower-arch, jamb of tower-door, 75*, 76*; font, aisle, 76; shallow transept, 168; general view of church, 172*; pinnacle, 173*; window, 176*.
Meneage, district of, 44; derivation of, 44, 60.
Merthen, remains at, 108.
Michael Penkivel, St., church of, 163.
Michael's Mount, St., "St. Michael's Chair" on, 173.
Mullion, St., 54—60; crucifix, corbel-head, 55*; stoup, 56*; bench-end, arms of the Passion, 56*, 57*; font, 58; carving on the altar, 58*; tablet in chancel, 59; openings at junction of chancel and nave, 92; crockets, 178; pinnacle, 179*.

Paul, St., 31—38; parish register, 32; arch between nave and aisle, 34*; windows, 34; tower, 35*; belfry windows, 36*; mural monuments, 36; tower, 172.
Pendinas, landing of Irish saints at, 1.
Perran-uthnoe, St., 116, 121—124; corbel of tower-arch, keystone of south doorway, figure of St. James the Great, 123*; shafts, capitals, 179.
Piran's, St., oratory, 163, 165.

Porth-curnow, ancient chapel at, 21, 141*.
Probus, St., tower of, 162.

Rosemoddress, stone circle at, 200.
Ruan Major, St., 89—95; window in south aisle, 90*; carving on roodscreen, triangular notching, 91; plan of church, 92*; openings at junction of chancel and nave, 93*; tower, 94*; cross, 181*.
Ruan Minor, St., 95—97; piscina, 96*; font, 97*; general view of church, 174*.

Samson, kistvaen, 234*.
Sancreed, 38—40; panels of roodscreen, 39*; pinnacle, 170*; section of pier, 179*; impost, stoup, 181*.
Scilly Isles, Athelstan's expedition against, 2; kistvaen, Samson, 234*.
Sennen, St., 21—24; capital, 22*; roodscreen, font, 22; mutilated image of the Virgin, 24*; bells, 24; shafts, 179; impost, 181*; general view of church, 192*; section of pier, 194*.
Shevioke Church, 163.
Sithney, St., 158.

Towednack, 148—151; general view of church, mouldings of tower, 149*; plan of tower stairs, incised stone, 150*.
Trembath, ancient cross, 187*.
Trewoofe, manor-house, 205; doorway, 206*.

Wendron, St., 98—108; plan of church, 99; moulding of mural-arch, chancel and transept, 100; east window of chancel, 101*; east window of transept, capital of pier, 102*; section, capital, and base mouldings of aisle piers, 103; section of hood-moulding, piscina in aisle, 104*; font, capping of tower buttresses, 105*; belfry rhyme on tower, 105; brass of Warin Penallinyk, incised stone, 107*; porch, 177.

Zennor, 151—156; plan of church, 151; Norman window, 152*; doorway, chancel, transept, 153; section of hoodmould, transept window, window in chancel, 154*; shallow transept, 168.

A SELECTION FROM RECENT PUBLICATIONS OF
JAMES PARKER AND CO.
OXFORD, AND 6 SOUTHAMPTON-STREET, STRAND, LONDON.

Devotions for the Sick.

THOUGHTS ON PASSAGES OF HOLY SCRIPTURE for the Sundays and Chief Holy Days of the Christian Year. Designed primarily for SICK PERSONS, whose illness incapacitates them from attending Church. By EDWARD MEYRICK GOULBOURN, D.D., D.C.L. (formerly Dean of Norwich). Crown 8vo., cloth, 5s.

(Uniform with "HISTORY OF THE CHURCH OF ENGLAND, FOR SCHOOLS AND FAMILIES.")

History of the Church Catholic.

By the Rev. A. H. HORE, M.A., of Trinity College, Oxford; Author of "History of the Church of England," &c. Crown 8vo., cloth, price 6s.

History of the Church of England,

FOR SCHOOLS AND FAMILIES. By the Rev. A. H. HORE, M.A., Trinity College, Oxford. New Edition. Crown 8vo., cloth, 552 pp., 5s.

A History of the Early Formularies

OF FAITH OF THE WESTERN AND EASTERN CHURCHES, to which is added an Exposition of the Athanasian Creed; being the Substance of a Course of Lectures by the Rev. CHARLES A. HEURTLEY, D.D., the Lady Margaret Professor of Divinity, and Canon of Christ Church, Oxford. Crown 8vo., cloth, price 4s. 6d.

Supplement to "Notes of My Life" (1879) and "Mr. Gladstone" (1886).

By the Ven. Archdeacon DENISON, Vicar of East Brent. 8vo., cloth, price 7s. 6d.

Meditations on the Life of Christ.

By THOMAS A KEMPIS. Newly discovered and fully authenticated. Third Edition, with the original Preface by the late Rev. S. KETTLEWELL, D.D. Fcap. 8vo., cloth, 5s.

A Glossary of Heraldry.

A Glossary of Terms used in Heraldry. A New Edition with One Thousand Illustrations. Post 8vo., cloth, 10s. 6d.

The Seven Sayings from the Cross:
ADDRESSES by WILLIAM BRIGHT, D.D., Canon of Christ Church, Oxford. Fcap. 8vo., limp cloth, 1s. 6d.

Lays of the Early English Church.
By W. FOXLEY NORRIS, M.A., Rector of Witney. Fcap. 8vo., cloth, with Twelve Illustrations, 3s. 6d.

A Harp from the Willows.
By Rev. W. MOORE, Author of "Lost Chords," "Periculis Urbis." Fcap. 8vo., cloth, 3s.

The Administration of the Holy Spirit
IN THE BODY OF CHRIST. The Bampton Lectures for 1868. By the late LORD BISHOP OF SALISBURY (Moberly). Third Edition. Crown 8vo., 7s. 6d.

An Explanation of the Thirty-Nine Articles.
By the late A. P. FORBES, D.C.L., Bishop of Brechin. With an Epistle Dedicatory to the Rev. E. B. PUSEY, D.D. New Edition, in one vol., Post 8vo., 12s.

A Short Explanation of the Nicene Creed,
For the Use of Persons beginning the Study of Theology. By the late A. P. FORBES, D.C.L., Bishop of Brechin. New Edition, Crown 8vo., cloth, 6s.

The History of Confirmation.
By WILLIAM JACKSON, M.A., Queen's College, Oxford; Vicar of Heathfield, Sussex. Crown 8vo., cloth, 2s. 6d.

Addresses to the Candidates for Ordination
On the Questions in the Ordination Service. By the late SAMUEL WILBERFORCE, LORD BISHOP OF WINCHESTER. Fifth Thousand. Crown 8vo., cloth, 6s.

On Eucharistical Adoration.
With Considerations suggested by a Pastoral Letter on the Doctrine of the Most Holy Eucharist. By the late Rev. JOHN KEBLE, M.A., Vicar of Hursley. 24mo., sewed, 2s.

The Catholic Doctrine of the Sacrifice
And Participation of the Holy Eucharist. By GEORGE TREVOR, M.A., D.D., Canon of York; Rector of Beeford. Second Edition, revised and enlarged. Crown 8vo., cloth, reduced to 5s.

DOCTRINAL THEOLOGY.

S. Athanasius on the Incarnation, &c.

S. Patris Nostri S. Athanasii Archiepiscopi Alexandriæ de Incarnatione Verbi, ejusque Corporali ad nos Adventu. *Greek Text* with an English *Translation* by the Rev. J. RIDGWAY, B.D., Hon. Canon of Ch. Ch. Fcap. 8vo., cloth, 5s.

St. Cyril on the Mysteries.

The Five Lectures of St. Cyril on the Mysteries, and other Sacramental Treatises; *Greek Text* with *Translations*. Edited by the Rev. H. DE ROMESTIN, M.A., Great Maplestead, Essex. Fcap. 8vo., cloth, 3s.

S. Aurelius Augustinus, EPISCOPUS HIPPONENSIS,

De Catechizandis Rudibus, de Fide Rerum quæ non videntur, de Utilitate Credendi. A New Edition, with the Enchiridion. Fcap. 8vo., cloth, 3s. 6d.

Translation of the above.
Cloth, 3s. 6d.

Διδαχὴ τῶν δώδεκα 'Αποστόλων.

The Teaching of the Twelve Apostles. The *Greek Text* with English *Translation*, Introduction, Notes, and Illustrative Passages. By the Rev. H. DE ROMESTIN, Incumbent of Freeland, and Rural Dean. Second Edition. Fcap. 8vo., cloth, 3s.

The Apology of Tertullian for the Christians.

Translation, with Introduction, Analysis, and Appendix containing the Letters of Pliny and Trajan respecting the Christians. By T. HERBERT BINDLEY, M.A., Merton College, Oxford. Crown 8vo., cloth, 3s. 6d.

The Pastoral Rule of S. Gregory.

Sancti Gregorii Papæ Regulæ Pastoralis Liber, ad JOHANNEM, Episcopum Civitatis Ravennæ. *Latin Text* with an English *Translation*. By the Rev. H. R. BRAMLEY, M.A., Fellow of Magdalen College, Oxford. Fcap. 8vo., cloth, 6s.

Vincentius Lirinensis.

For the Antiquity and Universality of the Catholic Faith against the Profane Novelties of all Heretics. *Latin Text* and English *Translation*. New Edition, Fcap. 8vo., 3s.

De Fide et Symbolo:

Documenta quædam nec non Aliquorum SS. Patrum Tractatus. Edidit CAROLUS A. HEURTLEY, S.T.P., Dom. Margaretæ Prælector, et Ædis Christi Canonicus. Editio Quarta, Recognita et Aucta. Crown 8vo., cloth, 4s. 6d.

Translation of the above.
Cloth, 4s. 6d.

The Canons of the Church.

The Definitions of the Catholic Faith and Canons of Discipline of the First Four General Councils of the Universal Church. *Greek Text* and English *Translation*. Fcap. 8vo., cloth, 2s. 6d.

The Athanasian Creed.

A Critical History of the Athanasian Creed, by the Rev. DANIEL WATERLAND, D.D. Fcap. 8vo., cloth, 5s.

The English Canons.

The Constitutions and Canons Ecclesiastical of the Church of England, referred to their Original Sources, and Illustrated with Explanatory Notes, by MACKENZIE E. C. WALCOTT, B.D., F.S.A., Præcentor and Prebendary of Chichester. Fcap. 8vo., cloth, 2s. 6d.

Studia Sacra:

Commentaries on the Introductory Verses of St. John's Gospel, and on a Portion of St. Paul's Epistle to the Romans; with an Analysis of St. Paul's Epistles, &c., by the late Rev. JOHN KEBLE, M.A. 8vo., cloth, 10s. 6d.

Discourses on Prophecy.

In which are considered its Structure, Use and Inspiration. By JOHN DAVISON, B.D. Sixth and Cheaper Edition. 8vo., cloth, 9s.

The Worship of the Old Covenant

CONSIDERED MORE ESPECIALLY IN RELATION TO THAT OF THE New. By the Rev. E. F. WILLIS, M.A., late Vice-Principal of Cuddesdon College. Post 8vo., cloth, 5s.

A Summary of the Evidences for the Bible.

By the Rev. T. S. ACKLAND, M.A., late Fellow of Clare Hall, Cambridge; Incumbent of Pollington cum Balne, Yorkshire. 24mo., cloth, 3s.

A Plain Commentary on the Book of Psalms

(Prayer-book Version), chiefly grounded on the Fathers. For the Use of Families. 2 vols., Fcap. 8vo., cloth, 10s. 6d.

The Psalter and the Gospel.

The Life, Sufferings, and Triumph of our Blessed Lord, revealed in the Book of Psalms. Fcap. 8vo., cloth, 2s.

The Study of the New Testament:

Its Present Position, and some of its Problems. AN INAUGURAL LECTURE delivered on Feb. 20th and 22nd, 1883. By W. SANDAY, M.A., D.D., Dean Ireland's Professor of the Exegesis of Holy Scripture. 64 pp. 8vo., in wrapper, 2s.

Sayings Ascribed to Our Lord

By the Fathers and other Primitive Writers, and Incidents in His Life narrated by them, otherwise than found in Scripture. By JOHN THEODORE DODD, B.A., late Student of Christ Church, Oxford. Fcap. 8vo., cloth, 3s.

A Commentary on the Epistles and Gospels in the Book of Common Prayer.

Extracted from Writings of the Fathers of the Holy Catholic Church, anterior to the Division of the East and West. With an Introductory Notice by the DEAN OF ST. PAUL'S. 2 vols., Crown 8vo., cloth, 10s. 6d.

Catena Aurea.

A Commentary on the Four Gospels, collected out of the Works of the Fathers by S. THOMAS AQUINAS. Uniform with the Library of the Fathers. A Re-issue, complete in 6 vols., cloth, £2 2s.

A Plain Commentary on the Four Holy Gospels,

Intended chiefly for Devotional Reading. By the Very Rev. J. W. BURGON, B.D., Dean of Chichester. New Edition. 4 vols., Fcap. 8vo., limp cloth, £1 1s.

The Last Twelve Verses of the Gospel according to S. Mark

Vindicated against Recent Critical Objectors and Established, by the Very Rev. J. W. BURGON, B.D., Dean of Chichester. With Facsimiles of Codex ℵ and Codex L. 8vo., cloth, 6s.

The Gospels from a Rabbinical Point of View,

Shewing the perfect Harmony of the Four Evangelists on the subject of our Lord's Last Supper, and the Bearing of the Laws and Customs of the Jews at the time of our Lord's coming on the Language of the Gospels. By the late Rev. G. W. PIERITZ, M.A. Crown 8vo., limp cloth, 3s.

Christianity as Taught by S. Paul.

By the late W. J. IRONS, D.D., of Queen's College, Oxford; Prebendary of S. Paul's; being the BAMPTON LECTURES for the Year 1870, with an Appendix of the CONTINUOUS SENSE of S. Paul's Epistles; with Notes and Metalegomena, 8vo., with Map, Second Edition, with New Preface, cloth, 9s.

S. Paul's Epistles to the Ephesians and Philippians.

A Practical and Exegetical Commentary. Edited by the late Rev. HENRY NEWLAND. 8vo., cloth, 7s. 6d.

The Explanation of the Apocalypse.

By VENERABLE BEDA, Translated by the Rev. EDW. MARSHALL, M.A., F.S.A., formerly Fellow of Corpus Christi College, Oxford. 180 pp. Fcap. 8vo., cloth, 3s. 6d.

A History of the Church,

From the Edict of Milan, A.D. 313, to the Council of Chalcedon, A.D. 451. By WILLIAM BRIGHT, D.D., Regius Professor of Ecclesiastical History, and Canon of Christ Church, Oxford. Second Edition. Post 8vo., 10s. 6d.

The Ecclesiastical History of the First Three Centuries,

From the Crucifixion of Jesus Christ to the year 313. By the late Rev. Dr. BURTON. Fourth Edition. 8vo., cloth, 12s.

A Brief History of the Christian Church,

From the First Century to the Reformation. By the Rev. J. S. BARTLETT. Fcap. 8vo., cloth, 2s. 6d.

A Brief History of the English Church.

By ALFRED CECIL SMITH, M.A., Vicar of Summertown, Oxford. Fcap. 8vo., limp cloth, 2s. 6d.

The Church in England from William III. to Victoria.

By the Rev. A. H. HORE, M.A., Trinity College, Oxford. 2 vols., Post 8vo., cloth, 15s.

A History of the English Church,

From its Foundation to the Reign of Queen Mary. By MARY CHARLOTTE STAPLEY. Fourth Edition, revised, with a Recommendatory Notice by DEAN HOOK. Crown 8vo., cloth, 5s.

St. Paul in Britain;

Or, The Origin of British as opposed to Papal Christianity. By the Rev. R. W. MORGAN. Second Edition. Crown 8vo., cloth, 2s. 6d.

The Sufferings of the Clergy during the Great Rebellion.

By the Rev. JOHN WALKER, M.A., sometime of Exeter College, Oxford, and Rector of St. Mary Major, Exeter. Epitomised by the Author of "The Annals of England." Second Edition. Fcap. 8vo., cloth, 2s. 6d.

Missale ad usum Insignis et Præclaræ Ecclesiæ Sarum.
Ed. F. H. DICKINSON, A.M. A few Copies of Parts II., III., and IV., price 2s. 6d. each, may still be had to complete sets.

The First Prayer-Book of Edward VI. Compared
With the Successive Revisions of the Book of Common Prayer. Together with a Concordance and Index to the Rubrics in the several Editions. Second Edition. Crown 8vo., cloth, 12s.

An Introduction
TO THE HISTORY OF THE SUCCESSIVE REVIsions of the Book of Common Prayer. By JAMES PARKER, Hon. M.A. Oxon. Crown 8vo., pp. xxxii., 532, cloth, 12s.

The Principles of Divine Service;
Or, An Inquiry concerning the True Manner of Understanding and Using the Order for Morning and Evening Prayer, and for the Administration of the Holy Communion in the English Church. By the late Ven. PHILIP FREEMAN, M.A., Archdeacon of Exeter, &c. 2 vols., 8vo., cloth, 16s.

A History of the Book of Common Prayer,
And other Authorized Books, from the Reformation; with an Account of the State of Religion in England from 1640 to 1660. By the Rev. THOMAS LATHBURY, M.A. Second Edition, with an Index. 8vo., cloth, 5s.

The Prayer-Book Calendar.
THE CALENDAR OF THE PRAYER-BOOK ILLUSTRATED. (Comprising the first portion of the "Calendar of the Anglican Church," with additional Illustrations, an Appendix on Emblems, &c.) With 200 Engravings from Medieval Works of Art. Sixth Thousand. Fcap. 8vo., cl., 6s.

A CHEAP EDITION OF
The First Prayer-Book
As issued by the Authority of the Parliament of the Second Year of King Edward VI. 1549. Tenth Thousand. 24mo., limp cloth, price 1s.

Also,
The Second Prayer-Book of Edward VI.
Issued 1552. Fifth Thousand. 24mo., limp cloth, price 1s.

Ritual Conformity.
Interpretations of the Rubrics of the Prayer-Book, agreed upon by a Conference held at All Saints, Margaret-street, 1880—1881. Third Edition, 80 pp. Crown 8vo., in wrapper, 1s.

The Ornaments Rubrick,
ITS HISTORY AND MEANING. Fifth Thousand. 72 pp., Crown 8vo., 6d.

The Catechist's Manual;

By EDW. M. HOLMES, Rector of Marsh Gibbon, Bicester. With an Introduction by the late SAMUEL WILBERFORCE, LORD BP. OF WINCHESTER. 6th Thousand. Cr. 8vo., limp cl., 5*s.*

The Confirmation Class-book:

Notes for Lessons, with APPENDIX, containing Questions and Summaries for the Use of the Candidates. By EDWARD M. HOLMES, LL.B., Author of the "Catechist's Manual." Second Edition, Fcap. 8vo., limp cloth, 2*s.* 6*d.*
THE QUESTIONS, separate, 4 sets, in wrapper, 1*s.*
THE SUMMARIES, separate, 4 sets, in wrapper, 1*s.*

Catechetical Lessons on the Book of Common Prayer.

Illustrating the Prayer-book, from its Title-page to the end of the Collects, Epistles, and Gospels. Designed to aid the Clergy in Public Catechising. By the Rev. Dr. FRANCIS HESSEY, Incumbent of St. Barnabas, Kensington. Fcap. 8vo., cloth, 6*s.*

Catechising Notes on the Apostles' Creed;

The Ten Commandments; The Lord's Prayer; The Confirmation Service; The Forms of Prayer at Sea, &c. By A WORCESTERSHIRE CURATE. Crown 8vo., in wrapper, 1*s.*

The Church's Work in our Large Towns.

By GEORGE HUNTINGTON, M.A., Rector of Tenby, and Domestic Chaplain of the Rt. Hon. the Earl of Crawford and Balcarres. Second Edit., revised and enlarged. Cr. 8vo., cl. 3*s.* 6*d.*

Notes of Seven Years' Work in a Country Parish.

By R. F. WILSON, M.A., Prebendary of Sarum, and Examining Chaplain to the Bishop of Salisbury. Fcap. 8vo., cloth, 4*s.*

A Manual of Pastoral Visitation,

Intended for the Use of the Clergy in their Visitation of the Sick and Afflicted. By A PARISH PRIEST. Dedicated, by permission, to His Grace the Archbishop of Dublin. Second Edition, Crown 8vo., limp cloth, 3*s.* 6*d.*; roan, 4*s.*

The Cure of Souls.

By the Rev. G. ARDEN, M.A., Rector of Winterborne-Came and Author of "Breviates from Holy Scripture," &c. Fcap. 8vo., cloth, 2*s.* 6*d.*

Questions on the Collects, Epistles, and Gospels,

Throughout the Year. Edited by the Rev. T. L. CLAUGHTON, Vicar of Kidderminster. For the Use of Teachers in Sunday Schools. Fifth Edition, 18mo., cl. In two Parts, *each* 2*s.* 6*d.*

Tracts for the Christian Seasons.

FIRST SERIES. Edited by JOHN ARMSTRONG, D.D., late Lord Bishop of Grahamstown. 4 vols. complete, Fcap. 8vo., cloth, 12s.

SECOND SERIES. Edited by JOHN ARMSTRONG, D.D., late Lord Bishop of Grahamstown. 4 vols. complete, Fcap. 8vo., cloth, 10s.

THIRD SERIES. Edited by JAMES RUSSELL WOODFORD, D.D., late Lord Bishop of Ely. 4 vols., Fcap. 8vo., cloth, 14s.

Short Readings for Sunday.

By the Author of "Footprints in the Wilderness." With Twelve Illustrations on Wood. Third Thousand, square Crown 8vo., cloth, 3s. 6d.

Faber's Stories from the Old Testament.

With Four Illustrations. New Edition. Square Crown 8vo., cloth, 4s.

CATECHISMS, &c., by the late Rev. C. S. GRUEBER,
Vicar of S. James, Hambridge, Diocese of Bath and Wells.

The Church of England the Ancient Church of the Land.

Its Property. Disestablishment and Disendowment. Fate of Sacrilege. Work and Progress of the Church, &c., &c. A CATECHISM. Fourth thousand, 24mo., limp cloth, 1s.

Holy Order.

A CATECHISM. 220 pp. 24mo., in wrapper, 3s.

A Catechism on the Church, The Kingdom of God:

For the Use of the Children of the Kingdom. Fourth thousand, 280 pp. 24mo., limp cloth, 2s.

"Is Christ Divided?"

On Unity in Religion, and the Sin and Scandal of Schism, That is to say, of Division, Disunion, Separation, among Christians. A CATECHISM. 8vo., in wrapper, 1s.

The Catechism of the Church of England

Commented upon, and Illustrated from the Holy Scriptures and the Book of Common Prayer, with Appendices on Confirmation, &c., &c. Third thousand, 24mo., limp cloth, 1s.

For a Series of Parochial Books and Tracts published by Messrs. Parker, see the Parochial Catalogue.

Oxford Editions of Devotional Works.

Fcap. 8vo., chiefly printed in Red and Black, on Toned Paper. Also kept in a variety of Leather Bindings.

Andrewes' Devotions.
DEVOTIONS. By the Right Rev. LANCELOT ANDREWES. Translated from the Greek and Latin, and arranged anew. Cloth, 5s.

The Imitation of Christ.
FOUR BOOKS. By THOMAS A KEMPIS. A new Edition, revised. Cloth, 4s.
Pocket Edition. 32mo., cloth, 1s.; bound, 1s. 6d.

Laud's Devotions.
THE PRIVATE DEVOTIONS of Dr. WILLIAM LAUD, Archbishop of Canterbury, and Martyr. Antique cloth, 5s.

Spinckes' Devotions.
TRUE CHURCH OF ENGLAND MAN'S COMPANION IN THE CLOSET. By NATHANIEL SPINCKES. Floriated borders, antique cloth, 4s.

Sutton's Meditations.
GODLY MEDITATIONS UPON THE MOST HOLY SACRAMENT OF THE LORD'S SUPPER. By CHRISTOPHER SUTTON, D.D., late Prebend of Westminster. A new Edition. Antique cloth, 5s.

Devout Communicant.
THE DEVOUT COMMUNICANT, exemplified in his Behaviour before, at, and after the Sacrament of the Lord's Supper: Practically suited to all the Parts of that Solemn Ordinance. 7th Edition, revised. Edited by Rev. G. MOULTRIE. Fcap. 8vo., toned paper, red lines, ant. cloth, 4s.

Taylor's Holy Living.
THE RULE AND EXERCISES OF HOLY LIVING. By BISHOP JEREMY TAYLOR. Antique cloth, 4s.
Pocket Edition. 32mo., cloth, 1s.; bound, 1s. 6d.

Taylor's Holy Dying.
THE RULE AND EXERCISES OF HOLY DYING. By BISHOP JEREMY TAYLOR. Ant. cloth, 4s.
Pocket Edition. 32mo., cloth, 1s.; bound, 1s. 6d.

Taylor's Golden Grove.
THE GOLDEN GROVE: A Choice Manual, containing what is to be Believed, Practised, and Desired or Prayed for. By BISHOP JEREMY TAYLOR. Antique cloth, 3s. 6d.

Wilson's Sacra Privata.
SACRA PRIVATA. The Private Meditations, Devotions, and Prayers of the Right Rev. T. WILSON, D.D., Lord Bishop of Sodor and Man. Now first Printed entire, from the Original Manuscripts. Antique cloth, 4s.

ΕΙΚΩΝ ΒΑΣΙΛΙΚΗ.
THE PORTRAITURE OF HIS SACRED MAJESTY KING CHARLES I. in his Solitudes and Sufferings. New Edition, with an Historical Preface by C. M. PHILLIMORE. Cloth, 5s.

Ancient Collects.
ANCIENT COLLECTS AND OTHER PRAYERS, Selected for Devotional Use from various Rituals, with an Appendix on the Collects in the Prayer-book. By WILLIAM BRIGHT, D.D. Fourth Edition. Antique cloth, 5s.

EUCHARISTICA:
Meditations and Prayers on the Most Holy Eucharist, from Old English Divines. With an Introduction by SAMUEL, LORD BISHOP OF OXFORD. A New Edition, revised by the Rev. H. E. CLAYTON, Vicar of S. Mary Magdalene, Oxford. In Red and Black, 32mo., cloth, 2s. 6d.—Cheap Edition, 1s.

DAILY STEPS TOWARDS HEAVEN;
Or, PRACTICAL THOUGHTS on the GOSPEL HISTORY, for Every Day in the Year. Compiled by ARTHUR H. DYKE TROYTE. 50th Thousand. 32mo., roan, 2s. 6d.; mor., 5s.
LARGE-TYPE EDITION. Crown 8vo., cloth antique, 5s.

THE HOURS:
Being Prayers for the Third, Sixth, and Ninth Hours; with a Preface and Heads of Devotion for the Day. Seventh Edition. 32mo., 1s.

PRIVATE PRAYERS FOR A WEEK.
Compiled by WILLIAM BRIGHT, D.D., Canon of Christ Church, Oxford. 96 pp. Fcap. 8vo., limp cloth, 1s. 6d.

By the same Author,
FAMILY PRAYERS FOR A WEEK.
Fcap. 8vo., cloth, 1s.

STRAY THOUGHTS:
For Every Day in the Year. Collected and Arranged by E. L. 32mo., cloth gilt, red edges, 1s.

OUTLINES OF INSTRUCTIONS
Or Meditations for the Church's Seasons. By the late JOHN KEBLE, M.A. Edited, with a Preface, by the late R. F. WILSON, M.A. 2nd Edition. Cr. 8vo., cloth, toned paper, 5s.

SPIRITUAL COUNSEL, ETC.
By the late Rev. J. KEBLE, M.A. Edited by the late R. F. WILSON, M.A. Fifth Edition. Post 8vo., cloth, 3s. 6d.

MEDITATIONS FOR THE FORTY DAYS OF LENT.
By the Author of "Charles Lowder." With a Prefatory Notice by the ARCHBISHOP OF DUBLIN. 18mo., cloth, 2s. 6d.

OF THE IMITATION OF CHRIST.
Four Books. By THOMAS A KEMPIS. Small 4to., printed on thick toned paper, with red border-lines, &c. Cloth, 12s.

PRAYERS FOR MARRIED PERSONS.
From Various Sources, chiefly from the Ancient Liturgies. Selected by C. WARD, M.A. Third Edition, Revised. 24mo., cloth, 4s. 6d.; Cheap Edition, 2s. 6d.

FOR THE LORD'S SUPPER.
DEVOTIONS BEFORE AND AFTER HOLY COMMUNION. With Preface by J. KEBLE. Sixth Edition. 32mo., cloth, 2s. With the Office, cloth, 2s. 6d.

A MENOLOGY;
Or Record of Departed Friends. 16mo., cloth, 3s.
[Arranged for recording the dates of the Death of Departed Relatives and Friends, a suitable Text being supplied for each day. Similar to Birthday-books.]

THE AUTHORIZED EDITIONS OF
THE CHRISTIAN YEAR,
With the Author's latest Corrections and Additions.

NOTICE.—Messrs. PARKER are the sole Publishers of the Editions of the "Christian Year" issued with the sanction and under the direction of the Author's representatives. All Editions without their imprint are unauthorized.

	s.	d.		s.	d.
Handsomely printed on toned paper. SMALL 4to. EDITION. Cloth extra . . .	10	6	32mo. EDITION. Cloth, limp . . . . Cloth boards, gilt edges .	1 1	0 6
DEMY 8vo. EDITION. Cloth	6	0	48mo. EDITION. Cloth, limp	0	6
FCAP. 8vo. EDITION. Cloth	3	6	Roan	1	6
24mo. EDIT. With red lines, cl.	2	6	FACSIMILE OF THE 1ST EDITION. 2 vols., 12mo., boards	7	6

The above Editions are kept in a variety of bindings.

By the same Author.

LYRA INNOCENTIUM. Thoughts in Verse on Christian Children. *Thirteenth Edition.* Fcap. 8vo., cloth, 5s.
———— 48mo. edition, limp cloth, 6d.; cloth boards, 1s.
MISCELLANEOUS POEMS by the Rev. JOHN KEBLE, M.A., Vicar of Hursley. *Third Edition.* Fcap. cloth, 6s.
THE PSALTER OR PSALMS OF DAVID: In English Verse. *Fourth Edition.* Fcap., cloth, 6s.

The above may also be had in various bindings.

By the late Rev. ISAAC WILLIAMS.

THE CATHEDRAL; or, The Catholic and Apostolic Church in England. Fcap. 8vo., cloth, 5s.; 32mo., cloth, 2s. 6d.
THE BAPTISTERY; or, The Way of Eternal Life. Fcap. 8vo., cloth, 7s. 6d. (with the Plates); 32mo., cloth, 2s. 6d.
HYMNS translated from the PARISIAN BREVIARY. 32mo., cloth, 2s. 6d.
THE CHRISTIAN SCHOLAR. Fcap. 8vo., cloth, 5s.; 32mo., cloth, 2s. 6d.
THOUGHTS IN PAST YEARS. 32mo., cloth, 2s. 6d.
THE SEVEN DAYS; or, The Old and New Creation. Fcap. 8vo., cloth, 3s. 6d.

CHRISTIAN BALLADS AND POEMS.

By ARTHUR CLEVELAND COXE, D.D., Bishop of Western New York. A New Edition, printed in Red and Black, Fcap. 8vo., cloth, 2s. 6d.—Cheap Edition, 1s.

The POEMS of GEORGE HERBERT.

THE TEMPLE. Sacred Poems and Private Ejaculations. A New Edition, in Red and Black, 24mo., cloth, 2s. 6d.—Cheap Edition, 1s.

REV. J. KEBLE.

SERMONS, OCCASIONAL AND PAROCHIAL. By the late Rev. JOHN KEBLE, M.A., Vicar of Hursley. 8vo., cloth, 12s.

REV. CANON PAGET.

THE REDEMPTION OF WORK. ADDRESSES spoken in St. Paul's Cathedral, by FRANCIS PAGET, M.A., Senior Student of Christ Church, Oxford. 52 pp. Fcap. 8vo., cloth, 2s.

CONCERNING SPIRITUAL GIFTS. Three Addresses to Candidates for Holy Orders in the Diocese of Ely. With a Sermon. By FRANCIS PAGET, M.A., Senior Student of Christ Church, Oxford. Fcap. 8vo., cloth, 2s. 6d.

THE LATE BISHOP OF SALISBURY.

SERMONS ON THE BEATITUDES, with others mostly preached before the University of Oxford; to which is added a Preface relating to the volume of "Essays and Reviews." New Edition. Crown 8vo., cloth, 7s. 6d.

THE BISHOP OF NEWCASTLE.

THE AWAKING SOUL. As sketched in the 130th Psalm. Addresses delivered at St. Peter's, Eaton-square, on the Tuesdays in Lent, 1877, by E. R. WILBERFORCE, M.A. [Rt. Rev., late Lord Bp. of Newcastle]. Crown 8vo., limp cloth, 2s. 6d.

VERY REV. THE DEAN OF CHICHESTER.

SHORT SERMONS FOR FAMILY READING, following the Course of the Christian Seasons. By the late Very Rev. J. W. BURGON, B.D., Dean of Chichester. First Series, 2 vols., Fcap. 8vo., cloth, 8s.—Second Series, 2 vols., Fcap. 8vo., cloth, 8s.

SERMON FOR CHRISTIAN SEASONS. First Series, edited by JOHN ARMSTRONG, D.D. 4 vols., fcap. 8vo., cloth, 10s.

—————— Second Series, edited by the Rev. JOHN BARROW, D.D. Fcap. 8vo., cloth, 10s.

The late Dr. Elvey's Psalter.

Just published, 16mo., cloth, 1s.; by Post, 1s. 2d.
A CHEAP EDITION (being the 20th) of
THE PSALTER; or, Canticles and Psalms of David.
Pointed for Chanting on a New Principle. With Explanations and Directions. By the late STEPHEN ELVEY, Mus. Doc., Organist of New and St. John's Colleges, and Organist and Choragus to the University of Oxford. With a Memorandum on the Pointing of the *Gloria Patri*, by Sir G. J. ELVEY.

Also,
II. FCAP. 8vo. EDITION (the 21st), limp cloth, 2s. 6d. With PROPER PSALMS. 3s.
III. LARGE TYPE EDITION for ORGAN (the 18th). Demy 8vo., cloth, 5s.
THE PROPER PSALMS separately. Fcap. 8vo., sewed, 6d.
THE CANTICLES separately (18th Edition). Fcap. 8vo., 3d.

The Psalter is used at St. George's Chapel, Windsor, and at many Cathedrals.

HISTORICAL TALES,

Illustrating the Chief Events in Ecclesiastical History, British and Foreign, &c.

Fcap. 8vo., 1s. each Tale, or 3s. 6d. each Volume in cloth.

ENGLAND. Vol. I.

1.—THE CAVE IN THE HILLS; or, Cæcilius Viriathus.
5.—WILD SCENES AMONGST THE CELTS.
7.—THE RIVALS: A Tale of the Anglo-Saxon Church.
10.—THE BLACK DANES.
14.—THE ALLELUIA BATTLE; or, Pelagianism in Britain.

ENGLAND. Vol. II.

16.—ALICE OF FOBBING; or, The Times of Jack Straw and Wat Tyler.
18.—AUBREY DE L'ORNE; or, The Times of St. Anselm.
21.—THE FORSAKEN; or, The Times of St. Dunstan.
24.—WALTER THE ARMOURER; or, The Interdict.
27.—AGNES MARTIN; or, The Fall of Cardinal Wolsey.

AMERICA AND OUR COLONIES.

3.—THE CHIEF'S DAUGHTER; or, The Settlers in Virginia.
8.—THE CONVERT OF MASSACHUSETTS.
20.—WOLFINGHAM; or, The Convict Settler of Jervis Bay.
25.—THE CATECHUMENS OF THE COROMANDEL COAST.
28.—ROSE AND MINNIE; or, The Loyalist: A Tale of Canada in 1837.

FRANCE AND SPAIN.

2.—THE EXILES OF THE CEBENNA; a Journal written during the Decian Persecution.
22.—THE DOVE OF TABENNA; and THE RESCUE.
23.—LARACHE: A Tale of the Portuguese Church in the Sixteenth Century.
29.—DORES DE GUALDIM: A Tale of the Portuguese Revolution.

EASTERN AND NORTHERN EUROPE.

6.—THE LAZAR-HOUSE OF LEROS: a Tale of the Eastern Church.
11.—THE CONVERSION OF ST. VLAdimir; or, The Martyrs of Kief.
13.—THE CROSS IN SWEDEN; or, The Days of King Ingi the Good.
17.—THE NORTHERN LIGHT: A Tale of Iceland and Greenland.
26.—THE DAUGHTERS OF POLA; a Tale of the Great Tenth Persecution.

ASIA AND AFRICA.

4.—THE LILY OF TIFLIS: a Sketch from Georgian Church History.
9.—THE QUAY OF THE DIOSCURI: a Tale of Nicene Times.
12.—THE SEA-TIGERS: A Tale of Mediæval Nestorianism.
15.—THE BRIDE OF RAMCUTTAH: A Tale of the Jewish Missions.
19.—LUCIA'S MARRIAGE; or, The Lions of Wady-Araba.

THE PENNY POST,

A Monthly Periodical devoted to the furtherance of Church Principles.

The oldest of the Penny Church Magazines.

FORTY-SIXTH YEAR OF ISSUE.

Containing Tales, Short Articles on visits to well-known Historical Spots in Great Britain, Occasional Historical Articles, Biographical Sketches, Poetry, Notes on Books, &c.

THE EDITOR'S BOX, for asking and answering questions relating especially to Church matters, is continued as formerly,

**32 Pages, Demy 8vo., Price One Penny.
Four or Five Illustrations in every Number.**

Works of the Standard English Divines,
PUBLISHED IN THE LIBRARY OF ANGLO-CATHOLIC THEOLOGY.

Andrewes' (Bp.) Complete Works. 11 vols., 8vo., £3 7s.
    THE SERMONS. (Separate.) 5 vols., £1 15s.

Beveridge's (Bp.) Complete Works. 12 vols., 8vo., £4 4s.
    THE ENGLISH THEOLOGICAL WORKS. 10 vols., £3 10s.

Bramhall's (Abp.) Works, with Life and Letters, &c.
5 vols., 8vo., £1 15s.

Bull's (Bp.) Harmony on Justification. 2 vols., 8vo., 10s.
—————— **Defence of the Nicene Creed.** 2 vols., 10s.
—————— **Judgment of the Catholic Church.** 5s.

Cosin's (Bp.) Works Complete. 5 vols., 8vo., £1 10s.

Crakanthorp's Defensio Ecclesiæ Anglicanæ. 8vo., 7s.

Frank's Sermons. 2 vols., 8vo., 10s.

Forbes' Considerationes Modestæ. 2 vols., 8vo., 12s.

Gunning's Paschal, or Lent Fast. 8vo., 6s.

Hammond's Practical Catechism. 8vo., 5s.
————— **Miscellaneous Theological Works.** 5s.
————— **Thirty-one Sermons.** 2 Parts. 10s.

Hickes's Two Treatises on the Christian Priesthood.
3 vols., 8vo., 15s.

Johnson's (John) Theological Works. 2 vols., 8vo., 10s.
—————— **English Canons.** 2 vols., 12s.

Laud's (Abp.) Complete Works. 7 vols., (9 Parts,) 8vo., £2 17s.

L'Estrange's Alliance of Divine Offices. 8vo., 6s.

Marshall's Penitential Discipline. 8vo., 4s.

Nicholson's (Bp.) Exposition of the Catechism. (This volume cannot be sold separate from the complete set.)

Overall's (Bp.) Convocation-book of 1606. 8vo., 5s.

Pearson's (Bp.) Vindiciæ Epistolarum S. Ignatii.
2 vols., 8vo., 10s.

Thorndike's (Herbert) Theological Works Complete.
6 vols., (10 Parts,) 8vo., £2 10s.

Wilson's (Bp.) Works Complete. With Life, by Rev. J. KEBLE. 7 vols., (8 Parts,) 8vo., £3 3s.

    ⁎ *The* 81 *Vols. in* 88, *for* £15 15s. *net.*

By Subscription.

A NEW SERIES
Of English Translations of the more Important Writings of
The Nicene and Post-Nicene Fathers.

ISSUED in conjunction with the "Christian Literature Company" of New York.

Subscription—One Guinea, payable previous to the issue of each *two* Volumes, each Volume consisting of 500 to 600 Quarto pages. The Volumes will be delivered as they appear free of carriage to all Subscribers giving an address in Oxford, Cambridge, London, Edinburgh, and Dublin. To other addresses the *postage* will be at the rate of 9*d*. per Volume, to be sent at the time of sending the Subscription.

    I. EUSEBIUS OF CÆSAREA [died A.D. 340].—Church History.—Life of Constantine the Great.—Oration of Constantine.
    II. SOCRATES [died after A.D. 439].—Church History.
        SOZOMEN [died A.D. *c*. 450].—Church History.
    III. THEODORET [died A.D. 458].—Church History.—Dialogues.—Letters.
        JEROME AND GENNADIUS, Lives of Illustrious Men.
        RUFINUS, Life and Works, with Jerome's Apology against Rufinus.
    IV. ATHANASIUS [died A.D. 373].—Against the Heathen.—On the Incarnation.—On the Opinion of Dionysius.—Life of Antony, &c.
    V. GREGORY OF NYSSA [died A.D. 395].—Against Eunomius.—Great Catechetical Oration.—On the Soul and the Resurrection.—On Virginity.—On the Holy Trinity.—On the Making of Man.—Against Macedonius.—Letters.
    VI. JEROME [died A.D. 419].—Commentaries.—Letters, &c.

The above 6 volumes, issued under the Editorial Supervision of HENRY WACE, D.D., *and* PHILIP SCHAFF, LL.D., *may be had at Three Guineas for the set of Six Quarto Volumes, and on receipt of Three Guineas will be sent immediately.*

Those who take the first 6 Volumes will be entitled to receive the remainder at the rate of One Guinea for each 2 Volumes as issued.

    VII. CYRIL OF JERUSALEM [died A.D. 388].—Catechetical Lectures.
        GREGORY OF NAZIANZUM [died A.D. 391].—Orations.—Sermons, &c.
                                                              [*Issued.*
    VIII. BASIL [died A.D. 379].—On the Holy Spirit.—Select Letters. [*Issued.*
    XI. SULPITIUS SEVERUS [died after A.D. 420].—Life of S. Martin of Tours.—Letters.—Dialogues.
        VINCENT OF LERINS [died A.D. 450].—Commonitory on the Rule of Faith.
        JOHN CASSIAN [died A.D. *c*. 490].—Collations of the Fathers. [*Issued.*
    XII. LEO I. [died A.D. 451].—Select Epistles.—Sermons.
        GREGORY I. [died A.D. 604].—Pastoral Theology.—Letters. Pt. 1.
                                                               [*Just issued.*

The following are in course of Issue,

    IX. HILARY OF POITIERS [d. A.D. 368].—On the Trinity.—On Synods.
    X. AMBROSE [died A.D. 397].—On the Holy Spirit.—Letters.—Hymns.
    XIII. JOHN OF DAMASCUS [d. A.D. 754].—Exposition of Orthodox Faith.
    XIV. EPHRAEM SYRUS [died A.D. 379].—Select Commentaries.—Homilies.—Hymns.

Prospectus and Specimen free on application to
JAMES PARKER and CO., Booksellers, 27 Broad Street, Oxford.

www.ingramcontent.com/pod-product-compliance
Lightning Source LLC
Chambersburg PA
CBHW032133230426
43672CB00011B/2324